A PACIFIST IN TROUBLE

A PACIFIST IN TROUBLE

BY

WILLIAM RALPH INGE

Essay Index Reprint Series

BOOKS FOR LIBRARIES PRESS
FREEPORT, NEW YORK

First Published 1939
Reprinted 1971

INTERNATIONAL STANDARD BOOK NUMBER:
0-8369-2192-5

LIBRARY OF CONGRESS CATALOG CARD NUMBER:
75-152176

PRINTED IN THE UNITED STATES OF AMERICA

CONTENTS

5

CONTENTS

6

CONTENTS

MISCELLANEOUS

INTRODUCTION

I CANNOT expect that this collection of *causeries*, written during the last eighteen months, in which the generosity of the *Evening Standard* allowed me to say nearly all that I wished to say, will be as kindly received as its predecessors. For I have done my puny and ineffectual best in the cause of peace—peace with Germany. I shall be accused of wishing to save some of my money for my children, and of sympathy with Nazism. The first is true; I am not ashamed of it, since I do not think that it influenced my judgment. The second is not true. As an old Victorian, I am in favour of freedom, peace and retrenchment. As a disciple of Plato, I believe that the rule of a dictator (*tyrannos* is his word) is the worst of all governments, and unlimited democracy the next worst. With Aristotle, Cicero, St. Thomas Aquinas, Burke and Lecky, I should prefer to live under a mixed government, like the late lamented British Constitution.

But I cannot forget that those who for years past have shrieked themselves hoarse in denouncing the iniquities of fascism, looked on with callous indifference or fiendish complacency while the Russian Bolsheviks butchered or deliberately starved to death eight or ten million persons, and while the Spanish Reds massacred 300,000 men and women

9

for no other crime than belonging to the middle class or being attached to the Catholic Church. When I think of the 16,000 bishops, priests, monks and nuns who were martyred for their faith in Spain, and who went gallantly to their deaths with "Long live Jesus Christ the King" on their lips, I cannot think much of the Christians at home who called their murderers by the absurd name of Loyalists, and encouraged hundreds of foolish boys to fight and die for these enemies of God and man. I do not think that the Russophil socialists who goaded our Government into attacking a nation which had no wish to quarrel with us care much either for liberty or humanity. They hate the dictators because they have borrowed and improved upon the technique of Sovietism. They see that the totalitarian states have abolished class warfare and united whole nations in an ardent and self-sacrificing patriotism. This is odious to a party which has long been known as the friend of every country except its own, and which has taught the wage-earners to regard the State—that is, the taxpayers who have been deprived of effective representation—as the universal provider. The owners of property under the dictators are worse off than they have been with us till the outbreak of the present war; but politics under fascism is something one degree better than competitive mass bribery. This is a poor set-off against the evils of a grinding tyranny—the hateful doctrine that reasons of State justify any crime; the

shameless aggression and perfidy; the cruel persecution of victimized races or classes; the suppression
of free speech, free writing, and public discussion;
the vile system of universal espionage and delation,
and all the other iniquities of an omnipotent and
unscrupulous government. It is another question
whether we shall convince the Germans of their
errors by shooting their men and bombing their
towns.

Peace is the first, second and third interest of this
country. We have nothing to gain by war and
everything to lose. If we are beaten—that does not
bear thinking of. If the war ends in a stalemate, we
shall have ruined ourselves for nothing. If we wear
down the Germans, the world will no doubt be rid of
the neurotic Hitler; his unhappy country will
probably be torn by civil war and revolution. But
twenty-five years hence we may find Germany
stronger and more aggressive than ever; or—and
I think this more likely—we shall wonder what
possessed us to break down the one effective barrier
against the domination of Europe and Asia by
Russia. Wars to maintain the balance of power have
no finality. We opposed the ambitions of Philip II,
Louis XIV, Napoleon, Nicholas I and Wilhelm II;
but security is as far off as ever, and our insular
immunity against attack is no more. Whatever may
be the issue of this war, we shall be too poor to
maintain a strong Navy. The only sea power in the
world will be the United States. Our Dominions, if

they are threatened, will appeal to America. Our little island will join the *ci-devant* Great Powers— Spain, Holland and Sweden. Such is the penalty for meddling and muddling in matters which do not concern us. The time is out of joint; but we were not born to set it right; we are not strong enough to do so.

This war should have been avoided and might ʰave been avoided, because the peoples in all the belligerent countries earnestly desired peace. The reception which the Prime Minister had at Munich and Rome was spontaneous and enthusiastic. Some who know Germany well have said that pacifism in Germany was really stronger than in the western democracies. This was not so in 1914, when the whole German nation was keyed up in the joyful expectation of a short and glorious war. The frightful experience of the Great War was not entirely thrown away, though a generation has grown up which does not remember those terrible years, and the old soldiers are very reticent about horrors which they wish to forget. It is a monstrous thing that young men should be sent to the shambles against the better judgment of the large majority. A leading psychologist has spoken of the inevitable return of manic-depressive insanity. But it is perhaps rash to argue from pathological states of the individual to the reaction of a society to an appeal to pugnacity or patriotism.

I am not afraid that the Germans will "dominate

the world by force," as the Prime Minister said. They are nearly bankrupt already, and as for the notion that they are made stronger by the annexation of new provinces, they will find themselves with several Irelands on their hands. For the Germans have an unique power of making themselves hated as well as feared, and the Slavs have long memories. The Czechs are likely to be peculiarly troublesome, for they sent several thousand volunteers to fight for the Spanish Communists. Theirs was the largest foreign contingent in the Red army, after those of the French and the Russians.

If the war ends in a stalemate or a German defeat, the seven millions who voted Communist not many years ago will probably show that they have not changed their minds. In England and France the middle class is strong enough to resist being "liquidated"; but in Germany the middle class was proletarianized by the inflation; some of the victims might even join in the revolution. The only country which is immune against Communism is Russia, which is convalescing after a severe attack of the disease.

Sooner or later Germany will have to settle accounts with Russia. The quarrel between Teuton and Slav is many centuries old. In 1914 the Germans maintained that they went to war solely in this cause. So they did; but the French, eager to recover their lost provinces, dragged us after them into what they had turned into a world war. So the

Slavs were saved. But the conflict must be renewed in the east of Europe. The Red Tsars will be as aggressive as the Romanoffs, and far more efficient. Time is entirely on the side of the Slavs. Which countries made most progress in the twenty years between the two wars? Czechoslovakia, Jugoslavia, Bulgaria and Rumania (which dislikes being called Slav). Even Russia, under an atrocious government, has made progress in some directions, such as education.

I ask my readers to consider the following statistics of population. The figures are for 1930, except in the case of Russia, and they are calculated, as usual, per thousand inhabitants.

	Births	Deaths	Surplus
Russia (1926) .	40·8	21·8	19·0
Rumania .	35·0	19·4	15·6
Poland .	32·8	15·8	17·0
Bulgaria .	30·6	15·8	14·8
Germany .	17·5	11·1	6·4

In 1933 the German figures were 14·7; 11·2; 3·5. I shall be reminded that the German birth-rate has increased since the Nazis came into power. Great pressure has been brought by the Government, through rewards and penalties, to produce this result, and the birth-rate has been raised to 19, as compared with 35·6 in 1900. The German *Frau* will not be bullied into producing unlimited food

14

for powder to please Herr Hitler. The abnormally low birth-rates under the Weimar republic were the result of extreme despondency and demoralization. They were achieved largely by means of abortion. Carr Saunders says that in Berlin in 1929 the proportion of abortions to live births was 103·4 to 100. What the French call *le vice allemand* was also rampant, and practised without concealment.

The Germans say they need *Lebensraum*. This is romantic nonsense. The true birth-rate of Germany (I have explained this matter in one of the articles in this book) is hardly more than enough to keep the population stable. But the Poles, as Bismarck complained, multiply like rabbits.

So much for the political aspect of the crisis, as it appears to me. But what ought a Christian to think about war? Ought he to condemn it absolutely, and to form societies who refuse to take any part in it? This is the opinion of Aldous Huxley, who regards war as a purely abominable thing. War is mass murder organized in cold blood. It blocks every road towards a better state of society. Instead of ensuring the survival of the fittest, it eliminates the strong and spares the unhealthy. Buddhism and Hinduism forbid even laymen to fight, or to have anything to do with the manufacture of arms. Wars never end war; they end in an unjust peace and a war of revenge. Individuals can do much as propagandists against violence, and against the passions which lead to violence.

Bertrand Russell—no Christian, but a born rebel —goes further still. He thinks that the cause of peace needs martyrs. When a sufficient number of men have been shot as cowards or traitors for refusing to bear arms, public opinion will come round to their point of view. So in history the persecution under Diocletian collapsed because it was felt even by the pagans to be unjust, and the spectacular victory of the Church followed a few years later. I respect those who could accept this kind of martyrdom, but, to bring the matter to a test, I should not like a son of mine to face a firing-party rather than fight for his country. There are limits to the right of private judgment. And yet the time will come when the world will honour the grave of the unknown soldier who died in the cause of peace.

There have been several societies of war-resisters, even in Germany, with periodicals such as *Die Friedenswarte* and *Die Eiche*. It is needless to ask what has become of them now. When Lord Ponsonby in 1927, as Under-Secretary for Foreign Affairs, submitted to the Prime Minister a Peace Letter signed by 128,770 persons who pledged themselves to refuse military service, his movement was taken up so eagerly in Germany that by the end of the year 137,000 persons had signed the pledge in Rhineland and Westphalia alone.

What is the teaching of Christianity about war? Only a very brief answer can be given in this Introduction. The Gospel of Jesus Christ condemns war and violence absolutely. In the Old Testament there are two currents, one pacific (cf. Isa. ix. 1–6 and xi. 1–9; Ps. xlvi and Zech. ix. 9, 10), the other fiercely militarist and ultra-patriotic. The latter gained the upper hand, and at last drove the nation to its ruin. About the teaching of Christ there can be no doubt whatever (cf. Matt. v. 43–5, Luke ix. 51–6 and other passages).[1] The Christian ethic, says Harnack, excludes all violence and absolutely rules out war.

It is said that Christ used military similes, and so tacitly accepted war. He also compared the coming of the Son of Man to that of a house-breaker (Matt. xxiv. 42), without intending to encourage burglary. Nor is it legitimate to say that the ethics of the gospel are determined by the erroneous belief in an impending apocalypse. If this view is accepted, we must abandon the attempt to base our conduct on the teaching of Christ. It is, however, true that the early Christians felt themselves to be "strangers and pilgrims upon earth," and that the reform of institutions was as little in their minds as it was in their power.

The question of service in the army did not press upon the early Church. The army was comparatively small, and there was no conscription. But towards the close of the second century patriotic Romans thought that the existence of a large

---

[1] The quibble that "love your enemies" refers only to private feuds is inadmissible. The distinction between ἐχθρός and πολέμιος does not apply to N.T. Greek, where πολέμιος is never used.

society of conscientious objectors might be a public danger. The lost treatise of Celsus undoubtedly contained an appeal to Christians not to refuse to help the Empire in a time of danger. But until the fourth century the attitude of Christian writers is uncompromising. Justin Martyr, the heretic Marcion, Origen, Tertullian, Cyprian, Lactantius and Eusebius all denounce war as incompatible with Christianity. Towards the end of this period there were many executions of Christians who, after their conversion, refused to remain in the army. One of them, Maximilian, was canonized by the Church.

After the conversion of Constantine, and indeed a little earlier, there was a great change. The Council of Arles in A.D. 314 excommunicated those who deserted the colours for conscience sake. Christians had become too numerous and influential, and the peril of the Empire too obvious, to make the early aloofness from public affairs any longer possible. A State religion cannot maintain that affairs of State are not its business. A very grave ethical problem was thus raised.

Substantially, the solution, so far as a solution was arrived at, was as follows. The Stoics had laid stress on the Law of Nature—absolute ethics, and the Church accepted this doctrine, adding that the Law of Nature was interpreted by the Law of Christ. But the absolute Law of Nature knows nothing of the State, of criminal jurisdiction, nor of war, institutions which exist in human society, or, as the

Christians said, in a state of sin. The Church, it was said, must accept a relative Law of Nature which is binding on all citizens under the present dispensation. Those who wished to make no accommodation with a sinful world were encouraged to become monks or hermits. Athanasius, Ambrose and the immensely influential Augustine, all justify wars of self-defence. Pope Leo, about A.D. 455, pronounced that military service may be embraced without guilt.

The Christian conscience has never been at ease about this concession. From the Montanists to the Lollards and Quakers there have been groups, mostly belonging to what Troeltsch calls the sect-type, who have thought themselves bound by literal obedience to the teaching of Christ and His early disciples. A double standard of morality is a thing which they have refused to accept.

Since the teaching of Augustine was on the whole that of the Mediæval Church, we may pass on to the Reformation. Luther accepted the double standard; but, instead of assigning the two moralities to different classes of people, the "religious" and Christians "in the world," he taught that all Christians must acknowledge the ethics of the Sermon on the Mount, which should regulate their personal conduct, and the State morality, in support of which he appeals to the Old Testament. With his habitual brutality he says, "The hand which bears the sword is no longer man's hand, but God's.

It is not man, but God, who hangs, breaks on the wheel, beheads, strangles and makes wars." The effect of this teaching on the German nation has been disastrous. Calvin rejected Lutheran dualism, but his full acceptance of the Old Testament made him blind to what was most distinctive in the teaching of Christ. He justified war, as Luther did.

In the Anglican Article xxxvii, it is laid down that the Christian, "at the command of the magistrate," may wear weapons and serve in the wars. The word *iusta* before *bella* has disappeared in the English version.

But the age of the Reformation produced at least one noble protest against war—from the pen of Erasmus: "Nothing is more impious, more calamitous, more inveterate, more base, or in sum more unworthy of a man, not to say of a Christian, than war. It is worse than brutal; to man no wild beast is more destructive than his fellow-man. When brutes fight, they fight with weapons which Nature has given them, whereas we arm ourselves for mutual slaughter with weapons which Nature never thought of. Neither do beasts break out in hostile rage for trifling causes, but either when hunger drives them to madness, or when they find themselves attacked, or when they are alarmed for the safety of their young. But we, on frivolous pretences, what tragedies do we act in the theatre of war! Under cover of some obsolete and disputable claim to territory; in a childish passion for a mistress; for causes even more ridiculous than these, we kindle the flame of war. Transactions truly hellish are called holy wars. Bishops and grave divines, decrepit as they are in person, fight from the pulpit the battles of the princes, promising remission of sins to all who will take part in the war of the prince, and exclaiming to the latter that God will fight for him, if he only keeps his mind favourable to the cause of religion. And yet how could it ever enter into our hearts that a Christian should imbrue his hands in the blood of a Christian! What is war but murder and theft committed by great numbers on great numbers? Does not the Gospel declare in decisive words that we must not revile those who revile us, that we should do good to those who use us ill, that we should pray for those who design to take away our lives? The man who engages in war by choice is a wicked man; he sins against Nature, against God, and against man, and is guilty of the most aggravated and complicated impiety."

Among modern Lutherans who have preached the double morality we may mention Naumann, who says: "Both are necessary to life, the mailed fist and the hand of Jesus. Only upon this foundation is the higher morality of the gospel to be realized. This sounds hard and cruel, but it seems to me to be soundly Lutheran." Yes, it is, and soundly devilish.

The Catholic Church, in consecrating chivalry, made another concession to the world—this time to the pugnacious descendants of the northern invaders of the Roman Empire. The Templars were the Pope's janissaries.

Machiavelli shocked the world by proclaiming as accepted practice what the Italian cantons, including the Papacy, were doing to each other. It is more dangerous to preach what you practise than to practise what you preach. The Church in 1552 put Machiavelli on the Index, but continued to act on his principles.

The complete rejection of all moral and humane restraints is no new thing. Thucydides has branded the ruthlessness of the Greeks during the Peloponnesian War in an immortal chapter. In early modern times, after the murderous wars of religion, war became less cruel and destructive when it was carried on by small professional armies. Mercenaries enjoy plunder and rape, but they are not eager to kill or be killed. Modern conscription, which properly belongs only to a slave-state, has made war far more brutal, and it may be a logical extension of this brutality that one of the objects of war is now the massacre of non-combatants.

Napoleon produced Hegel, Fichte and Treitschke, as Clemenceau produced Hitler. The deification of race and country, the worship of the god-state, the glorification of war, are the reaction of a proud nation to what it regards as unjust humiliation. The real Germany, the land of the great philosophers, poets, musicians and scholars, seems for the present to be completely submerged, but it is difficult to believe that a nation to which civilization owes so much is permanently sunk in barbarism. The perversion has undoubtedly been made more terrible by the doctrine of a dual morality, as preached by Luther and Lutheran theologians.

The problem of a relative law of conduct is, however, very difficult. Can we condemn all acts of aggression? Ought the English to have left the Britons in possession of our island? Ought America to have been left to the Redskins, and Australia to the black-fellows? Has the white man any right to be in Africa? Now that the swarming period of the European peoples has come to an end, while their possessions are still half empty, is it right to keep the Chinese and Japanese out of California and Queensland? Universal disarmament would mean the economic victory of the cheap races in all under-populated countries. Or if we say that no doubt iniquitous aggressions were perpetrated in the past, but that we have repented of our evil ways, will it not be said, as it is said in many countries, that our pacifism is a desire to maintain the existing map of the world? A gambler who after a succession of successful coups proposes to play for love for the rest of the evening cannot expect to be listened to with gravity.

It is only honest to ask these questions, and to own that some of them are difficult to answer. But if as Christians we are bound to be pacifists, it need not trouble us that under a less misguided government we should be under no temptation to be otherwise. The British Commonwealth is a real league of nations in being, a new experiment, and one of the most interesting in history. Whatever may be thought of some of our actions in the past, we have a clear conscience now. And as for immigration, I cannot admit that countries with an unregulated birth-rate have a right to overrun the territories of their neighbours. The Americans, and the inhabitants of our Dominions, are trying the experiment of a civilization with a high standard of living. The experiment may succeed or it may fail; but they cannot be expected to allow it to be ruined by an influx of rice-eating Asiatics.

What are the prospects of peace in the future? We all hoped that the ghastly lesson of the Great War would be enough. But there is always danger when a generation grows up who have not known war at first hand. There is also a permanent danger from the military advisers of the Government, who are apt to assume that war must come sooner or later, and that it is for them to consider whether the chances of victory would be increased or diminished by delay. To this must be added the activities of politicians and diplomats who, like shady solicitors, hold out the threat of an action at law to reinforce chicanery. We, I believe, are the least guilty of the Great Powers in this respect.

Nothing that has been said about the folly and

wickedness of this terrible institution, the curse of the human race, must be taken to detract in the slightest degree from the admiration and gratitude which we all feel for the brave men who risk and often lose their lives in the service of their country. If there were not a noble side to war, the indignation of mankind would have swept it away long ago. It is to the honour of human nature that the appeal for self-sacrifice is stronger than all the self-regarding instincts. We must never say or think that our gallant boys died in vain. Their cause was sanctified by their devotion; their reward is with their God; their place is among the noble army of martyrs.

The other articles in this little book range over a wide variety of subjects, and need no introductory remarks. It is a satisfaction to me to restore to them their proper titles, though I should hope that no one who reads them could suppose that I had anything to do with the substituted headlines.

W. R. INGE.

BRIGHTWELL MANOR
WALLINGFORD
November, 1939.

THE WORLD WE LIVE IN

I

SOME SACRED BOOKS

CHRISTIANITY is not a religion of a book. If its Founder had wished it to be a religion of a book, He would have written or dictated the book Himself. But it was not His will that a line should go down to posterity stamped with His authority. Except on one occasion, when He traced we know not what characters on the unrecording earth, He made no use of the discovery of writing.

His disciples collected what they could remember of His teaching, and in course of time the Church possessed a sacred Book, the New Testament, which in the Anglican Church is the final court of appeal. It is a book of inestimable value.

After some hesitation, the Church adopted, as inspired by God, the patriotic literature of the ancient Hebrews. We could not be without the Old Testament, but there have been times in Church history when it has been used with too little discrimination. It has sometimes been quoted in support of bad causes, such as slavery, belief in witchcraft, and ferocious patriotism. "This is the book," says a Mediæval epigram, "where everyone seeks his own opinions, and where everyone finds his own opinions."

Whether the Turks have been encouraged to

read the Koran since the accession to power of the late Kemal Ataturk, I do not know; the Sultans did not favour its circulation in the Osmanli language. But in most Mohammedan countries boys are made to learn large portions of it by heart. It is believed to be verbally inspired, and has been used in magic almost from the first.

It is opened at random by persons seeking guidance, and quite lately the ordeal of compelling two litigants to drink water into which a verse of the Koran, with the ink still wet, had been dipped, was employed at Khartum.

The Koran is partly a kind of commonplace book of the Prophet, but its contents are so miscellaneous and chaotic that no brief description of them can be given. Isa (Jesus) is treated with great respect; we are told that He once made birds of clay and then brought them to life.

Very few persons, I imagine, have read the sacred books of the Latter Day Saints, as they call themselves. Joseph Smith, the founder of Mormonism, was "martyred" with his brother in 1844. The Book of Mormon, which he received, according to his own account, by direct inspiration, is a most amusing production, composed mainly in Old Testament diction, but mixed with Americanisms and containing blunders in grammar and spelling.

The Latter Day Saints at one time made numerous converts from all parts of the world, attracted, it may be feared, by the "peculiar institution" of plural marriage. Federal law has now compelled them to abandon polygamy, and Utah admits "Gentiles" as well as "Saints."

Christian Scientists also have their Bible, the works of Mary Baker Eddy, extracts from which are engraved on the walls of some of their churches. I have not read them, so I will not attempt to describe them.

Hitler's *Mein Kampf* is seen in every house in Germany. It is imprudent not to have a copy. Many millions of copies have been sold, and it is neither a small book nor a cheap one. If Hitler keeps the profits he must be a rich man.

I have only lately read the book. It is a perfectly naïve revelation of the author's mind. At the time when he wrote it he was a fiery young patriot, bitterly wounded by the defeat of his country in the Great War, and moved by a kind of apostolic fervour to be the prophet of its recovery.

So far as I can see, there is no ground for saying that it is a violent threat to the democracies of the West. He has a great respect for our country and would welcome an alliance. But England is entangled with France, which "does not wish Germany to be a Power at all. England does not wish Germany to be a world Power. There is a great difference." He says he does not want tropical colonies: but "the confines of *das Reich* should include every German."

The political philosophy of the book is crude in

the extreme. Hitler believes in slogans, and is convinced that the only way to convince the best-educated nation in Europe is to scream at them like a parrot.

To begin with, his obsession about the Jews is insane. He reviles them in every chapter in language which would be ridiculous if its consequences were not so tragic. It is not generally known that the Kaiser shared his rabid antipathy:

"Grey told Herbert Fisher that the last time he saw the Kaiser, at a luncheon party, he began abusing the Jews, and when Grey tried to calm him down he replied, hissing with hatred, 'I tell you, Sir Edward, what ought to be done with the German Jews; they ought to be killed, killed, killed!'"

(*Diaries of John Bailey.*)

Parliament is "an absurd institution." "Speaking before such a body is really casting pearls before swine." "We must not be led away by the will-o'-the-wisp called freedom of the Press; the Government must keep control of that instrument of popular education." "Perhaps the pacifist idea is a good one when the man at the top has just made himself sole master of the world."

It is quite possible to argue in favour of one-man government and to hold that it is or may be more efficient than parliamentary democracy. But to pour scorn on one of the greatest and most successful experiments in politics is an insult to the intelligence of his readers.

32

"The future of a movement is dependent on the fanaticism and intolerance with which its adherents defend it as the one right course."

Hatred of the Jews is mixed up with hatred of Bolshevism, which he calls a Jewish conspiracy. It is true that many revolutionists have been Jews—Marx, Lassalle, Trotsky, Radek, Zinovieff, Bela Kun and others. Some Jews, however, have done pretty well under Capitalism. In any case, now that the Bolshevist leaders are dead, with Stalin's bullets in their skulls, this part of the German Bible needs revision. The new State Capitalism in Russia is not very unlike Hitler's own Nazism.

Another crazy fad is the theory of pure race—the Nordic superman. There are no pure races; and it happens that the nations which have done most in the world have been splendid mongrels, like the Greeks (Nordic and Mediterranean), the French and Germans (Nordic and Alpine), and the English.

Hitler heaps derision upon internationalism. But what is to happen when the Germans meet another nation which believes in its Divine right and sacred mission? A war of extermination between them?

Let us sum up Hitler's gospel. "We Germans have been chosen among all the nations of the earth; therefore we are punished for our iniquities. For we have mingled with the heathen, married their daughters, learned their works and worshipped their idols. So we have been given into the hands of our enemies.

"Do not we hate them, O National Socialism, that hate thee? Yea, we hate them with a perfect hatred. But we shall still possess the gate of our enemies. We shall bruise them with a rod of iron and break them in pieces like a potter's vessel. Our birth-rate is going up. If any man can number the sand of the sea, then shall our seed be numbered."

Did any nation ever talk in this style before? Why, yes. The Jews did.

December, 1938.

II

THE GROUP-MIND IN POLITICS

DR. WILLIAM BROWN, who, since the recent death
of Professor William McDougall, is probably our
leading psychologist, has sent me his new book on
psychological methods of healing. The most interesting part of it, to most people, will be the
account of his wonderful success in the treatment of
shell-shock and similar nervous disorders in the
Great War. Few men have done more to heal the
wounds of that terrible episode in our history.

I have long been interested in the claims of
spiritual healers, about which I am perhaps unduly
sceptical. Dr. Brown is not inclined to set limits to
the influence of mind over body; he does not think
that a hard line can be drawn between functional
and organic disease. We must not split up a unitary
organism into different faculties, or suppose that
mind and body are ever independent of each other.

Personally I am surprised at the respectful
language which he uses about Freud. I agree with
the late J. W. N. Sullivan, who, in his little book,
The Tyranny of Science, says: "I believe that Freud's
form of psycho-analysis is really as silly as it looks.
It is the name of science that secures for these
theories such attention as they get from intelligent
people who are not cranks."

The Œdipus complex is surely a nasty delusion, and I entirely refuse to believe that my dreams are any indication of my subconscious character. This, however, is not the subject of the present article. There are a few pages at the end of the book in which he surveys the present state of European politics from the point of view of a psychologist.

The group-mind must not be regarded as a mystical entity apart from the individuals who compose the group. We must not personify the State as a super-individual, or a god to whom all the citizens may be offered in sacrifice, nor must we personify Germany, Italy or Japan as female figures with mostly undesirable qualities. But it is true that persons acting as members of a group behave very differently, sometimes better, more often much worse, than they would do as isolated individuals.

The group usually forms itself round a leader, who is invested with ideal characteristics.

"Unfortunately, when individuals get together in a group under a leader, with reference to some particular policy or programme, the identification which takes place may have the effect of cancelling for the time being the higher mental powers which distinguish one person from another, leaving only the primitive instinctive tendencies. People acting in such a group act in a more primitive way than they would otherwise do. They are fickle, shallow and impulsive, and although for that reason often ineffective, at times they can produce momentarily overwhelming results."

Such groups within a nation may not be very serious, but when a feeling of crude nationalism is aroused and whipped up by the leaders, we have a regression to a more primitive attitude towards life which may be disastrous.

"That the extreme nationalist movement is regressive is obvious. It is because I am a psychologist that I have felt so unhappy about the attitude of the other nations towards the defeated Powers. We have been too slow in meeting our adversaries. We postponed any action to alleviate difficulties till it was too late."

Nationalism develops in poverty-stricken States of a belligerent type. Their natural pugnacity and national pride are intensified. Instead of living freely under the law, they place themselves deliberately under a dictator, who is never a man with wide liberal views. A dictator is never a liberal. Liberalism produces leaders who are men of peace, not men of war.

The same anti-liberal urge which produces militant nationalism is the moving force, according to Dr. Brown, in collectivism. Both violate the famous maxim of Kant: "Treat everyone as an end and never merely as a means."

Collectivism and nationalism both treat everyone as means to an end, the aggrandisement of a State or of an international system. That is a step back to a more primitive type. The whole tendency of Christianity, and of civilizations based upon it, has been towards the recognition of the inalienable rights of the individual and the sacredness of human personality. These are disregarded and often explicitly denied in the totalitarian States.

It is because the free nations have never risen to the height of their convictions, because they have not realized that freedom demands voluntary discipline and self-sacrifice, that the more primitive and essentially inferior types of organization seem by comparison so much more efficient.

Hence the real danger which threatens to overwhelm popular government wherever it still exists. If we are to remain free, we must be masters of ourselves. A nation that does not deserve freedom will soon lose it.

Dr. Brown's indictment of the conduct of the Allies after the Great War must be admitted. We were very unlucky in our representatives. Paris was the last city in which the conferences after the armistice ought to have been held. Clemenceau, "the tiger," dominated the situation. National passions had been stimulated to frenzy.

Take two examples only. I believe it is certain that both Masaryk and Beneš advocated the cession of the Sudeten-German area to Germany, but France and England objected to giving anything to the vanquished. King George V, as I know from a private source, expressed a hope that we should annex no territory after the War. How much wiser we should have been to follow his advice !

For some years after the War the Germans were in a subdued and almost penitent mood. We ought to have done everything to support the Weimar Republic, which stood for peace and reconciliation. Instead of doing so, we allowed the nation to seethe under a sense of injustice and humiliation, until the worst passions of the old Germany revived and produced the results which we see.

Could we have acted otherwise? Certainly we could if we had been better led. A hundred and twenty years ago the same problem presented itself, and was very differently handled. Our affairs were then in the hands of two men, Wellington and Castlereagh.

Wellington has been often misunderstood. He was a very great general who hated war and violence, and cared little for military glory. When a stranger helped him across the street, and said what a high honour it was to him to have been of use to the victor of Waterloo, the Iron Duke replied: "Don't be a d——d fool !"

As for Castlereagh, that much-maligned statesman, was there ever a more statesmanlike utterance than his letter to the Prime Minister, Lord Liverpool, who was in favour of harsher measures towards defeated France?

"It is not our business to collect trophies, but to bring back the world to peaceful habits. The more

I reflect upon it, the more I deprecate this system of scratching such a Power [as France]. We may hold her down and pare her nails so that many years shall pass away before she can again wound us.

"But this system of being pledged to a continental war for objects that France may one day reclaim from the particular States that hold them, without pushing her demands beyond what she would contend was due to her own honour is, I am sure, bad British policy."

If we had had Castlereagh and Wellington at Versailles, there would probably be no Hitler now. Perhaps Europe never committed a more expensive mistake than the Peace of Versailles. And, as Dr. Brown says, the remedy is a study of group psychology.

December, 1938.

III

WHO ARE THE JEWS?

THE official German doctrine of "race" and "blood" is the most grotesque piece of unscientific balderdash ever crammed down the throat of an intelligent people. The word "race" (not found in English before Foxe's *Book of Martyrs*) is now avoided by men of science, and "blood," in the literal sense, does not pass from mother to child, though Aristotle thought it did.

There is no Aryan race, though there are Aryan languages. There is no Jewish race, though there is a Jewish religion. A "nation" is a society united by a common error as to its origin and a common dislike and contempt for its neighbours.

A popular religion is a superstition which has enslaved a philosophy. A political slogan is a myth which has enslaved a science. The myth of a common ancestry has been very generally held by patriotic groups, and of course their own ancestors were the finest "race" in the world. The "Nordic race," distinguished by long heads, tall stature, blue eyes and yellow hair, are Nature's aristocrats. Unfortunately they tend to be swamped by the lesser breeds. *The Passing of the Great Race* is the title of an eloquent book written in the United States.

A few even of the old Greeks knew better. "Greece," said Isocrates, "is the name of a culture, not of a race." So we may be Greeks, though the sub-species which immortalized the name of Greece seems to have died out. The traveller in Greece to-day notices hardly any classical profiles. About one-quarter of the inhabitants of Southern Greece, I observed to my surprise, have blue or grey eyes and dark hair like the Irish. How did they get these?

"Let us make a composite picture of a typical Teuton," says Julian Huxley, "fair, long-headed, tall and virile. Let him be as blond as Hitler, as long-headed as Rosenberg, as tall as Goebbels, as slender as Goering, and as manly as Streicher. How much would he resemble the German ideal?"

Dürer's Germans have flat backs to their heads, like many modern Germans, and the greatest Germans, including Goethe, Kant (who had Scottish blood), Beethoven, Schiller and Leibniz, were all round-headed. Round heads indicate an Alpine, Armenoid or Tartar ancestry.

Over against the noble Nordics stand the wholly alien Jews, who, we are told, contaminate the pure blood of the ruling race. They must therefore be got rid of, and in the name of science they are being got rid of in no gentle fashion.

Well, who are the Jews? There is a very able paper on the "Ethnic Origins of the People of Palestine," by Canon Bridgeman, American chaplain at Jerusalem, in *Bible Lands* for January, 1939.

Semitic invaders entered Palestine before 3500 B.C. Non-Semitic Armenoid peoples filtered in later. The Armenoid head is flattened at the back, and the nose is very prominent, with a depressed tip and large "wings." The Hittite sculptures show this type, which is quite unlike the long-headed Bedouin skull.

The Israelites invaded this already mixed population about the same time that the Philistines, who probably came from Asia Minor, occupied the coast lands. The Israelites did not exterminate the natives, and their legislators forbade oppression. "The stranger that dwelleth with you shall be as one born among you, and thou shalt love him as thyself." "As ye are, so shall the stranger be before the Lord." Many an Israelite might hear from his neighbour: "Thy mother was a Hittite and thy father an Amorite."

The population of Palestine under the kings was partly Bedouin, partly Canaanite, and partly Armenoid, with a mixture of other strains.

The Assyrians deported most of the Ten Tribes in 720 B.C. They never returned, and foreigners from the East were brought in to replace them.

The Babylonians deported only the upper and middle classes, leaving the mainly Canaanite *fellahin* on the land.

The north was partly Hellenized under the successors of Alexander. The name of Gadara, to a classical scholar, suggests not a herd of swine, but the elegant love-poet Meleager and the Cynic philosopher Menippus. "Galilee of the Gentiles" was so mixed in ethnic types that the renegade Englishman, Houston Chamberlain, could suggest that Christ had probably no Jewish blood in his veins !

In the second and following centuries the population grew, and was largely Christianized. The Arab conquest in the seventh century brought in only a military aristocracy, but most of the native Christians embraced Islam and learned to speak Arabic. The "Arabs" in Palestine to-day are mainly the descendants of Byzantine Christians, and of the old "people of the land," Judeo-Canaanites.

The Jews of the Dispersion are of very mixed descent. They made many proselytes, including a large Turkish tribe, the Chazars, who were converted in the seventh century. I have seen one or two Jews with rather Mongoloid features.

It is usual to divide the Jews at the present day into the Sephardim, who are found chiefly in Southern Europe, and who as a rule look like the Mediterranean peoples, and the more numerous Ashkenazim, who are mostly broad-faced, like the Russians and Poles. It is clear that the Jews have taken the physical characteristics of the nations among whom they live. In other words, they have not kept their blood unmixed.

"The Jews are not a race," says Ripley in his book on the *Races of Europe*, and he is plainly right.

They are a religious and social group, whose habits have been determined mainly by the persistent ill-treatment which they have received.

But is there not a Jewish type of face? There is, and perhaps 30 per cent of Jews—I think not more —could be identified out of a crowd. In the same way we may find Englishmen, Frenchmen and Germans who could hardly belong to any other nation; but we should have to hunt for them. John Bull and Uncle Sam both exist, but we might pass days in London or New York without meeting them. Shylock exists also, but the Jews whom one meets are not much like him.

I may be reminded that I have spoken of Nordic, Mediterranean and Armenoid types. Are not these genuine races? Modern ethnologists prefer other names, such as "sub-species." But my point is that every national group is a mixture of some or all of these types, and that there is no proof that, for example, a pure Nordic, if we could find him, is a better man than the Mediterranean or Alpine. I have never seen a more typical Nordic head than the portraits of Kemal Ataturk. What was his family history?

There is nothing to choose between a long head and a broad head in the matter of brains. And though I certainly could not agree that there are no superior and inferior "races," it is ridiculous to allege that the Jews are in any way inferior to other Europeans. On the contrary, their average of talent is very high, especially in such intellectual fields as music, philosophy and natural science.

Perhaps it is good for a group to be hammered, if the hammering stops short of extermination. A list of distinguished men who are descended from French refugees would be very impressive.

Perhaps some of the refugees who are now coming to our shores from Germany and Austria may bring us equal fame—they themselves or their families. In any case, to expel them from Germany is an act of almost incredible stupidity as well as cruelty.

Irrational antipathies are difficult to combat, just because they are irrational. We may hope by degrees to "let the ape and tiger die," as Tennyson bids us. All very well, said Bishop Creighton; but we are still left with the donkey, a more intractable animal.

January, 1939.

IV

FACE THE FACTS

ARE the thoughts of a rustic moralist on the recent crisis likely to be worth reading? I do not know; but it is still difficult to turn our attention to any other subject.

It seems that we escaped by the skin of our teeth from a disaster which might have wrecked European civilization for a hundred years, and which would probably have ended finally the position of this country as one of the great Powers.

For let there be no mistake. France recovered from her defeat in 1870 in five years; Germany was as powerful as ever fifteen years after 1919. But our position is much more precarious. We should not recover from a crushing defeat.

And what were we going to fight about? The Germans wished to rectify, with characteristic brutality, an acknowledged mistake made at Versailles. The German part of Bohemia ought not to have been made part of a Slav republic.

The Sudeten Germans and the Czechs could live side by side while both were under the Austrian Government, because the Austrians are Germans; but to put Germans under a Czech Government was as great an insult as to annex Belfast to De

47

Valera's Eire. For the Germans regard Slavs as an inferior race.

We resented the manner in which the transfer was made, and rightly. Nevertheless, if the claim had been made in a less truculent way, it is certain that the French would have backed up the Czechs in refusing it.

We had no treaty with the Czechs, and no interest in their country, except our admiration for the noble Masaryk, one of the outstanding figures of our time. The alliance of France with Czechoslovakia was obviously part of her plan to encircle Germany, and this is no part of our policy.

Even the war of 1914, to help Serbia, was less remote from British interests than this war would have been. No one would have known what we were fighting about, and in spite of patriotic assertions to the contrary, nine out of ten Englishmen are strongly opposed to war.

We could have done nothing to help the Czechs, who as a conquered country would simply have been expunged from the map of Europe. I have not met any military authority who believes that an invasion of Germany from the West is a possible operation, even if Italy did not threaten the southern part of the French frontier.

The lunacy of the whole business was apparent even though war was averted. The greatest city in the world was to be evacuated, and its inhabitants scattered over the country. Gas masks were distributed to everybody, though they would have been useless against explosives and not of much use against mustard gas. Householders began digging trenches on their tennis courts.

I have always been opposed to our vague commitments—quite as dangerous as a formal alliance—with France. These commitments (called obligations of honour!) have twice brought us to imminent risk of destruction. For twenty-five years we have been dragged at the chariot-wheels of that ambitious Power, which has devoted friends at the Foreign Office.

But the last fortnight has shown, I think, that the French people are wiser than their rulers. Nothing has impressed me more than the enthusiastic welcome given in Paris to M. Daladier, and the almost unanimous approval of his action by the French Chamber.

For the French have suffered a resounding diplomatic defeat. Their ring of alliances against Germany has broken to pieces. The pact with Soviet Russia is probably at an end. Czechoslovakia is gone. The Jugoslavs must consult their own safety. France, except for our help, is isolated.

And yet the French are overjoyed to have escaped war. A friend of mine has just returned from France. Everywhere he found posters which were torn down by the police and put up again. They were headed, "*Nous ne voulons pas la guerre,*" and contained a pithy demonstration of the folly and futility of war. They were signed by about forty leading *royalists and socialists*.

This combination is most significant, as was the support of the Independent Labour Party to our Prime Minister.

On the evening when the agreement was announced, the name of Chamberlain was on everyone's lips in Paris. Streets were to be named after him. It is true that when the French heard that he and Hitler had signed a no-war pact, there was a grim silence, and murmurs of the old cry, "*Nous sommes trahis.*" But soon the question was asked, "Why should we not sign a similar pact? If the Germans do not wish to fight us, why should we not be friends?"

This no-war pact may be the most important outcome of the crisis. For the Germans do not want war on the West. They have certain ambitions in the East of Europe, which may possibly conflict with our interests in the future.

But if we wish to wage preventive wars, to stop some Continental nation from becoming too strong, we must scrap our social services and pile up an enormous army and fleet, although we have solemnly renounced war as an instrument of policy. We have made our choice, the right choice.

We must reconcile ourselves to the fact that if peace is the first interest of Great Britain, as it certainly is, we cannot prevent things being done by other nations which we think iniquitous.

We cannot police the world. To ride abroad re-dressing human wrongs may be all very well for Sir Lancelot; it only makes Don Quixote ridiculous. We are right to make our protests. But when we are snubbed for our pains it is no use to shake our fists and curse.

We are told that the whole of Eastern and South-Eastern Europe will soon fall into the orbit of Germany. I am very doubtful about this. Which nations of Europe have made most progress in population, wealth and culture since the war? Not the Germans, but the Slavs. Nations grow and decay during peace; war only registers these changes.

Japan may annex part of China, but in 100 years the invaders will be absorbed. They that take the sword shall perish by the sword, or, if not, they will learn that in this world nothing fails like success.

October, 1938.

V

NAZI ECONOMICS

I STRONGLY recommend a book called *The End of Economic Man*, by Dr. Peter Drucker, an eminent Austrian publicist and economist. The main thesis of the book is that Capitalism, Socialism and Communism, political creeds which all assume that man is first and foremost a money-getting and money-spending animal, have failed completely to establish a tolerable state of society.

Totalitarianism is a refuge of despair for a continent which has seen all its hopes wither. Either the countries still free must surrender to the "demon" of Fascism, or we must return to Christianity and humanism, with a quite different and non-economic standard of values.

Many outstanding intellectuals, as he shows, have come back to religion. He names Berdyaeff, formerly a Marxian; G. K. Chesterton, who began as a social reformer; Karl Barth, a member of the Socialist party; Bruening, a trade union secretary; Dostoevski, the Russian novelist; Pastor Niemoeller; and the Dane, Kierkegaard. The list might have been much longer, from Englishmen of letters alone.

I do not agree with everything in this book, but

the author gives his authority to some opinions which I have expressed myself.

"The demand for colonies is highly unpopular within Germany, and runs counter to Hitler's most cherished and most sensible foreign political goal —a lasting alliance between the British Empire and the German Empire." I wonder whether this is true?

"The masses, both in Italy and in Germany, are more afraid of war than the masses in the democracies."

"The Left Wing idea of a united front between the democracies and 'democratic' (!) Russia has done greater harm than all other political mistakes of the last twenty years. There must soon be an alliance between Russia and Germany. The two régimes are similar ideologically and socially. A Russo-German alliance is the only means by which both countries could overcome their economic and military difficulties." Internally, Russia is completely fascized. "It has become obvious that Marxist Socialism can only lead to an even greater inequality, to the complete loss of freedom and the emergence of a hereditary caste of officials as ruling class." "The European Left have not gained anything by shutting their eyes to this."

But to-day I wish to call attention to the very interesting chapter on Nazi economics. Like most of my generation, I was brought up on Mill's political economy, which teaches that a good citizen ought to eschew unproductive expenditure, and invest as much as possible of his income in productive enterprise, which gives employment and increases the wealth of the country.

This doctrine, which was correct, or at least natural, in a period of expansion, has now become most unpopular. Much more attractive for our generation is the theory which the Americans call "consumptionism." If we were all given plenty of money, and if we spent it all in buying things, trade would hum and we should all be happy. I have never believed in this theory, but it is what people like to believe, and some of our economists, as well as all our politicians, are willing to preach it.

Now Dr. Drucker shows that the totalitarian States, Russia and Germany, quite deliberately check consumption. The German labourer is not appreciably poorer than he was before the revolution, but he has to work longer hours and to pay taxes which would horrify the British working man. He is compensated partly by free holidays and excursions, and partly by complete social equality. In fact, the "peasant estate" is glorified as the "backbone of the race," and every town-bred boy or girl must spend a certain time as a worker on a farm.

The employer has no longer any freedom or control. He can neither hire nor dismiss a workman without a Government permit. He is told what wages to pay. Government orders must be executed below cost price. If any profits are made, the Government knows how to squeeze them back. There is no unemployment. The Nazis believe, like Mill, that only an increase in investment in capital goods can create employment. Depressions, they think, are caused by too much consumption and too little investment. Therefore, saving must be compulsory, and spending artificially reduced. This system was copied from Soviet Russia, which is financed by compulsory loans and compulsory "voluntary" contributions. The only difference is that in Russia forced savings are supposed to be applied to productive manufactures, in Germany they go to armaments. The Russian plan has failed, but then the Russian is probably the world's worst business man. Also, in Russia it is the peasants and unskilled workers whose standard of living has been artificially reduced; the bureaucracy live comfortably enough. But in Germany the burden is borne by the middle class. Not only are they heavily taxed, but meat, butter, eggs and milk are almost unprocurable. This compulsory under-consumption has released large sums for investment in Government loans. More than half of the annual national income is thus saved. All savings in banks, savings banks and insurance companies are forcibly invested in Government stock.

It is a mere assumption that armaments are economically more wasteful than the uses to which the capital expended upon them would have been put otherwise. Economically it is irrelevant whether money is used to buy wine or to make guns. We in England and America think that a high standard of consumption is desirable; but that has nothing to do with economics. Both Germany and Italy have officially given up the economic goal of an increased standard of living. "Guns instead of butter" is not an economic alternative; it is a social and moral choice.

The chief problem is how to get raw materials from other countries. This is solved largely by sheer bullying. Jugoslavia must supply copper and wheat; she has to take in exchange enough aspirin to provide every Jugoslavian with a pill every day. Greece must take tons of mouth organs for her tobacco and raisins. Bulgaria sends meat and tobacco, and receives in exchange a million artificial leather cameras without lenses.

I am not defending Nazism — far from it. I should not like to live in a country where a man who speaks his mind is sent to prison, his back scored by Gestapo whips. What interests me most is the repudiation of the theory of consumptionism, and the return to the doctrine of John Stuart Mill. If our modern theory is wrong, we are never likely to get rid of unemployment.

After all, under the new Budget we have gone a long way on the same road. The taxpayer will have to eat less butter, or to economize on some others of his little comforts. And we all earnestly hope that the guns will never be used. Dr. Drucker thinks that the Germans and Italians are at least equally keen that there shall be no war. Some demon seems to be driving us all to our own destruction. Is it a reversion to the cave-man, or shall we be old-fashioned enough to speak of the coming of Anti-christ?

The Germans and Italians have at rate put an end to the class war, and that is no small achievement.

May, 1939.

CHRISTIANITY IN MODERN LIFE

I

PEACE ON EARTH

"And suddenly there was with the angel a multitude of the heavenly host praising God, and saying, Glory to God in the highest, and on earth peace, good will to men." How shall we reconcile this promise with the sorrowful words of Christ Himself: "Think ye that I am come to bring peace on earth? I came not to bring peace, but a sword."

Of course these words do not describe Christ's will and intention. They prove only that He well knew the inevitable consequence of launching new ideas on the troubled sea of human history. Not peace, but division: division even within the same family, and much more between societies.

Family quarrels, persecutions, wars of religion, wars of ideas—must these things be? Human nature being what it is, they were sure to be. "It must needs be that offences come, but woe to the man by whom the offence cometh."

They would never have come, if Christians had understood their Master and His message better. For His method was never violence. "Violence is not an attribute of God," as a second-century Christian writer said. The method of Christ was always to begin with the human heart, and to work outwards from that.

His weapon was love or sympathy. He broke down all man-made barriers by ignoring them. In Christ, as St. Paul saw clearly, there is neither male nor female, neither Jew nor Aryan, neither German nor Englishman, neither Catholic nor Protestant; we are all one man in Christ Jesus.

"Peace I leave with you, my peace I give unto you. Not as the world giveth give I unto you." Not as the world giveth. In a sense, our peace is a war-like peace, and military metaphors have always been found appropriate by Christian teachers.

The Church does not exist merely to diffuse universal good nature. We have a definite ideal, social and individual, of how life ought to be lived, and those who try deliberately to make it impossible, and set up false gods in its place, must be our enemies, though "the weapons of our warfare are not carnal."

"We wrestle not against flesh and blood, but against the world-rulers of this darkness, against spiritual wickedness in heavenly places." Belief in evil spirits is not popular now, but we are confronted with something more formidable than human folly and weakness: Christianity is at grips with false ideals, and ideals have the terrible force of spiritual things.

The French historian Ozanam, writing in the nineteenth century, puts the matter admirably.

"There are two doctrines of progress. One, nourished in the schools of sensualism, rehabilitates the passions, and promising the nations an earthly paradise at the end of a flowery path, gives them only a premature hell at the end of a way of blood. The second, born from and inspired by Christianity, points to progress in the victory of the spirit over the flesh, promises nothing but as prize of warfare, and pronounces the creed which carries war into the individual soul to be the only way of peace for the nations."

This is the first lesson to be learned. There is a victory to be won in our own souls, by submitting ourselves to a discipline as strict as that of soldiers in war time. The harmony of the Christian character is a harmony of unified purposes, not of satisfied instincts.

The soul that is not master of itself soon loses its liberty. It cringes to the strong and bullies the weak. It sets up idols to worship—the State, or military glory, or some crazy theory about race or creed or class. Or else—and this is more common among ourselves—it has no clear ideal at all, and drifts in a devious course, carried away by shifting winds of doctrine.

"God, the author and lover of peace, whom to know is to live, whom to serve is to reign." So begins, in the terser Latin, one of our finest collects.

Such is the foundation of the character of the free Christian, who is the Lord's servant, the world's master, and his own man. And the peace that he has

63

won within he will seek for the world without. For he is delivered from fear, and fear is the chief cause of war and hatred and suspicion.

The angel's promise seems as far as ever from fulfilment. It has been long deferred, and hope deferred maketh the heart sick. We must not prophesy smooth things for ourselves or for our children.

There may be great troubles in store for us. We can see the tremendous force of a barbarous ideal when it seizes hold of a whole nation. But surely aggressive war is an anachronism, and sooner or later must be recognized as such.

It is a grievous thing that the country of Goethe and Schiller, of Kant and Hegel, of Handel and Beethoven, of Ranke and Mommsen should now be known only as the country of Hitler and Goebbels. But it is more grievous that the whole Christian world, after nearly two thousand years, should present the spectacle which we now see.

Is it not time that, instead of discussing whether Christianity is played out, we should agree to give it a trial?

How shall we, small people in a private station, best show that we, at any rate, believe that peace and good will have been offered us from heaven? There is one appeal which has been nobly responded to, and I do not think any of us could do better than give it our support, if we have not already done so. Those who cannot take the unhappy victims of persecution into their houses may send gifts of money to those who are administering the fund.

But I am sure of this, that we shall be wise not to say in print all that we think about this business. "The wrath of man worketh not the righteousness of God." There are those who wish to foment ill-will between the two nations, and who seize eagerly upon anything in the British Press which will arouse anger and hatred in Germany.

The German people are gagged and blindfolded. They do not know what is going on. Only the other day an intelligent German said to a friend of mine, "I want to go to England, but, of course, it would not be safe, while all this rioting is going on."

Rioting in England! But we must be careful not to suppose that everyone who has had the misfortune to be born between the Rhine and the Vistula has a double dose of original sin.

In 1870, during the war between France and Prussia, Dean Church gave this message on Christmas Day from the pulpit of St. Paul's:

"To-day bids us look up in spite of everything, and lift up our heads. Come what may, nothing can efface the mark which Christmas has made in the rolls of time. Let not private trouble, nor the march of the world and the clash of its conflicting powers, drown its holy call. It speaks to us if we will but listen; it speaks as it did on that first birthday of our Lord, of the peace beyond all understanding, of the joy unspeakable and full of glory, with which apostles and saints and martyrs went through life and death to God."

I should like to recall to my readers these words of my great predecessor in the Deanery. They are as true now as they were then.

December, 1938.

II

A RELIGION FOR WEAKLINGS?

SIR PHILIP GIBBS quotes in his book, *Across the Frontiers*, a very interesting conversation which he had with a prominent Nazi on the subject of Christianity.

"Christianity," said this Nazi, "is a weak kind of religion, very unscientific, very much out of touch with the realities of human nature, denying the joy of life.

"We don't believe in morbid asceticism and a divorce between mind and body. We believe in a new Trinity—Body, Mind and Spirit all working harmoniously and equally important.

"We want to produce a race of men and women . . . with healthy minds, regarding life not as a vale of tears but as a great adventure of joy.

"We want a new religion, more manly, not Oriental in its origin, not attempting to persuade young and healthy minds that a lot of old Jews in primitive times have anything to say to the modern world."

The charge that Christianity is a religion for slaves and weaklings is not new. Nietzsche, who created the portrait of the big blond beast roaring after his prey, thought that Christianity is a religion for "cows, sheep, dogs, Englishmen and other democrats."

Sir Philip Gibbs's acquaintance developed this idea in more restrained language.

Well, I have been reading another book which deals with this indictment against Christianity, Dr. Dixon's *The Human Situation*—the most readable course of Gifford Lectures ever written.

These lectures on natural religion, founded by Lord Gifford, have usually been very academic—either stiff philosophy, like mine on Plotinus, or (in recent years) pure natural science or unintelligible mathematics. The scientists make the Deity emerge unexpectedly, like a rabbit out of a hat, in the last lecture.

It was a happy thought of the University of Glasgow to appoint a professor of English Literature to lecture. "Divine philosophy" in his hands is "as musical as is Apollo's lute," and he has great fun with the pompous prophets of the nineteenth century. The book might be described as a series of raids, in which all the philosophers fare badly, except Leibniz.

Christianity, he thinks, is "evaporating into humanitarianism"—which, after all, we may murmur, is how it began in Galilee. But the Gospel, he says, was an Eastern and ascetic creed, a creed of withdrawal from life. Such a creed did not and could not convert Europe; Europe transformed it.

The fundamental impulse in all living creatures,

he thinks, is the will to live. Even the most convinced pessimists are in no haste to die. But the
will to live means the will to strive, to fight, often
to kill.

The harmony of life, as was said long ago, is a
harmony of opposite tensions, like a bow or a lyre.
Let us ask the question fairly. Would Adam and
Eve and their descendants have done better to stop
in the Garden of Eden and water their roses?
Would a farmyard of tame animals have been
interesting even to its Creator?

Of course we may run away from life if we like.
Many great teachers have recommended it. At one
time there were 37,000 houses of Benedictines alone,
not to speak of other brotherhoods. The wisdom of
the East on the whole recommends escape from life.
But what has Dame Nature to say to them? She is
not in the habit of talking, as Plotinus makes her
say; with her it is a word and a blow, and the blow
first. If you won't play my game, she says, you must
clear out.

But does Christianity counsel us to run away
from life? Not at all. It counters the selfish, brutal
will to live, not with the will to die, but with the
will to love, which after all is in Nature just as
essential as the will to live. It is the loveless man,
like Schopenhauer, who had all the intellectual
virtues and no others, who is the real pessimist, and
the real rebel against Nature.

Some very great men have been weak in human

sympathy, but it is a defect. Einstein confessed that "I have never belonged to my country, my home, my friends, or even my family with a whole heart." Not unnaturally he "regards individual existence as a sort of prison," and "longs to escape from personal life."

Spinoza was quite indifferent to the devastation of Central Europe in his time, and Plotinus says contemptuously that if people object to this sort of thing they ought to learn to fight better. None of these three was a Christian, and though no one could say that they have not deserved well of mankind, they were too much detached, by their intellectual interests, from human sympathies.

As for those who, as Bishop Creighton said, may be fit for heaven, but are of no earthly use, they have mistaken the purpose for which they were sent into the world.

"In nations," writes F. S. Oliver, "meekness is not a virtue, but a contemptible and very dangerous vice." What has Dame Nature, or Clio, the Muse of History, to say to that? Is Oliver right, or another guide who said: "They who take the sword shall perish by the sword"?

I will not quote another text, which I do not think was meant to be taken literally. When Mark Twain said: "The English are mentioned in the Bible: 'Blessed are the meek, for they shall inherit the earth,' " I am afraid he was laughing at us.

But in point of fact the "will to power," as the

Germans call it, has not been a success. We ourselves, like the Romans, collected an empire in a fit of absence of mind, and we are throwing it away in another fit of absence of mind. Most empires have died of severe indigestion.

This is not taking a very high line; but Dr. Dixon appealed to the law of the survival of the fittest. A much better answer is that it is the will to love, not the will to live, which is the parent of real heroism.

The pagans who called the Christians "a dingy, hole-and-corner tribe" (*tenebrosa et lucifugax natio*) little realized how love can transform poor, weak human nature. "He that loveth his brother" is not tempted to run away from life.

It seems to me that love or sympathy is the only motive which is strong enough to overcome selfishness without substituting for it something which may be still worse. As men are now constituted, a zeal sufficient to destroy selfishness is often worse than selfishness itself. Indoctrinated and collective virtue turns easily to fanaticism, the most cruel and destructive and irrational of all passions.

It is because Europe has been fanaticized that we cannot agree with Dr. Dixon that there has been a rapid growth of humanitarianism. Mercy is a tender plant which flourishes in cool climates.

September, 1938.

III

FREETHINKERS IN CONGRESS

THE proceedings in the Congress of the World Union of Freethinkers, held in London recently and reported in the *Rationalist Review*, fully justify the refusal of the Archbishop of Canterbury to join in an agitation to forbid the meeting. It was referred to in the Press as the anti-God congress; in reality it was what it professed to be, a conference of freethinkers. If it had been a meeting of dogmatic atheists, who disbelieve in God, no matter what anyone means by God, it would have been too high a compliment to them to try to prevent them from assembling.

The speeches were naturally affected by the international tension; but it was plain that most of the speakers were more anxious about the menace to liberty than about the first subject on the agenda, "the present religious reaction." The foreign delegates found a close connection between the two; in our country it would not be easy to do this.

The political and propagandist activities of the Roman Catholic Church were sharply attacked by the French and Belgian representatives. That this Church forbids its members to think for themselves is well known; it is not so plain that, as was said by these speakers, it is an ally of totalitarian dictators and an enemy of social reform. In fact, I think that these charges are untrue.

The Roman Church is an international political organization, like the Comintern. It is opposed to State-worship, and is therefore one of the chief obstacles to the new forms of absolutism. It may make concordats with governments, as in Italy; but Catholics can never renounce their primary allegiance to the papal theocracy.

As regards social reform, Catholicism has never accepted modern industrialism as Calvinism has done. It is most at home in simple agrarian communities. It is opposed to Communism, because Communism denies the "natural right" to private property—a right which, like other natural rights, may be forfeited by misuse; but it is not necessarily opposed to socialistic legislation.

A French speaker said that "Christian Socialism is a piece of Jesuitry, for it has no intention of attempting to carry out those reforms for which political Socialism stands." This is entirely untrue of Christian Socialism in this country.

The speakers at the Congress seem nearly all to belong to the Left Wing in politics. Christianity is an integral part of western civilization, and those who wish not to reform but to destroy our social order naturally regard the Churches, and not least the Liberal Churches, as their enemies. They are also right in thinking that there can be no reconciliation between secularism or "dialectical materialism"

73

and the Christian view of life. But one may be a freethinker without holding these views.

Two or three speakers dealt with religion and science. One of them naïvely supposed that Christians are still committed to the chronology of Archbishop Usher.

Professor Haldane deprecated the popular attempts to discredit science by calling attention to unsolved difficulties and contradictions. Here I think he was mainly right. Those who take refuge in gaps find themselves in a tight place when the gaps begin to close. This is an unworthy way of defending our faith.

Physicists do not try to slur over these difficulties. Is the electron a particle or a chain of waves? Is apparent "indeterminacy" real chance or unknown causation? Is the universe running down like a clock, or can the elements be built up as well as dissolved into radiation? There are several unsolved problems of great importance.

But we do not refute materialism by depriving "matter" of nearly all its properties. The onion can never be entirely peeled. Even if matter is only waves, there must be something which undulates.

When however Professor Haldane says that "all contradictions can eventually be solved by research on materialistic lines," he is being rashly overconfident. No one would repudiate such a statement more vigorously than the Professor's illustrious father, the late Professor John Haldane.

Biologists are still, with some exceptions, materialists; but I think other men of science, and almost all philosophers, would agree that materialism can never give us a closed system, a complete account of reality, because it is an abstract study of certain aspects only of the real world, leaving out other aspects which may be at least as important.

These speakers all reject Christianity. What would they give us in its place? Their own word would be "rationalism"; I should prefer "humanism." The two words are not synonymous; some humanists are not rationalists, and some rationalists, like the schoolmen, were orthodox Christians. Perhaps "secularism" would be a better word than either.

In practical matters, I agree with the American Professor Niebuhr when he says: "Christianity is right in rejecting purely rational ethics, but wrong when tempted to deny the validity of the rational contribution to ethics. There can be no social ethic for the common life without the contribution of reason."

I also think that traditional Christianity has been mistaken in substituting the word "supernatural" (which I should like to banish altogether) for St. Paul's word "spiritual." "First that which is natural, then that which is spiritual." Supernaturalism, I almost venture to say, is the mysticism of the materialist.

But what kind of guide is secularism? By what

standard does it bid us regulate our actions? "The greatest happiness of the greatest number"? This is a useful maxim; but what is happiness? Is it to have the maximum number of wants and the means of satisfying them? Or is it something that cannot be weighed or measured or counted at all?

The secularists have taken over much more than they realize from the long religious traditions which they have discarded, traditions which really depend on the belief that we are immortal spirits on our probation in a world which is not our final home.

Secularism has no standard except a vague utilitarianism, and if Christianity has been weak in influencing conduct, it is to be feared that secularism is much weaker.

I am more and more convinced, now that my life has been unfortunately prolonged into this wretched time, that nothing except the religion of Christ can save the world. By all means let the freethinkers go on thinking as freely as they like. "Where the Spirit of the Lord is, there is liberty."

But we think freely only when we think truly, and we think truly only when we know Him who is the Truth.

October, 1938.

76

IV

WILLIAM TYNDALE AND THE BIBLE

In the hall of Hertford College, Oxford, where I was a Fellow and Tutor for fifteen years, hangs a fine portrait of William Tyndale, one of the most estimable of the authors of the Protestant Reformation. There are two other extant portraits, one at Magdalen College, Oxford, the other in the house of the Bible Society; and there is a statue of him on the Victoria Embankment by Boehm, which was unveiled by Lord Shaftesbury in 1884.

Tyndale was born "on the borders of Wales," probably in Gloucestershire, about 1484. He studied at Oxford and Cambridge, and became a fine scholar, a master, we are told, of Greek, Latin, Hebrew, German, Spanish and French. This knowledge of languages was to stand him in good stead during his exile.

During a short residence in London as preacher at St. Dunstan-in-the-West, or while chaplain to a gentleman in his native county, he resolved to devote his life to translating the Bible into English.

It must not be supposed that this was a new thing. Aldhelm and Aidan, Bede and Alcuin, had been industrious translators. But their versions or paraphrases had ceased to be generally intelligible, and the history of the English Bible begins with

Wycliffe, whose disciples, the Lollards, were persecuted but not destroyed. Wycliffe's translation was
made from the Latin Vulgate; this could not satisfy
such a scholar as Tyndale.

He hoped to do his work in London under the
patronage of Bishop Tunstall; but he soon found
that "not only was there no room in my Lord of
London's palace to translate the New Testament,
but that there was no place to do it in all England."
So he went to Germany, first to Hamburg, from
which he is said to have visited Luther at Witten-
berg, then, hunted from pillar to post, to Cologne
and Worms.

Finally he found, as he hoped, a more secure
refuge at Antwerp, till he was betrayed to the
Emperor by an Englishman named Phillips, and
after a year's imprisonment was executed near
Brussels in October, 1536. He fared rather better
than his friend Rogers, who was burnt alive by
Queen Mary; for he was strangled before his
dead body was committed to the flames. His last
words were: "Lord, open the King of England's
eyes."

Tyndale entrusted his version of nearly all the
Old Testament and the whole of the New to Rogers,
who printed it with a dedication to the King, signed
Thomas Matthew. In this edition, which was
recommended by Cranmer to Thomas Cromwell,
part of the Old Testament was printed in Coverdale's translation, which in 1536 was ordered to be

placed in all churches. But the Archbishop recognized that Tyndale's version was better.

Thus Tyndale's New Testament, which had been publicly burnt a few years before, found its way into the churches and became the foundation of all subsequent translations. It was far superior to Coverdale's, which was made from the Vulgate.

In 1538–9 a few alterations were made in a new edition called the Great Bible, to which Cranmer wrote a preface.

Why, in these circumstances, was Tyndale persecuted, and why did the bishops hunt for his translation and burn it? Tyndale was certainly a Zwinglian —that is to say, he taught that the Communion is merely a service in memory of the death of Christ. This view is not permissible in the Church of England. Also, he was very acrimonious in controversy, and the prefaces which he prefixed to his translations were insulting to the hierarchy.

One of the most interesting documents of the Reformation period is his dispute with Sir Thomas More, who after favouring some kind of Erasmian reformation, turned back and wrote bitterly of his former friends. The two disputants were equal in ability, and, it must be confessed, in abusiveness. Controversies in those days were not conducted with rosewater.

But nothing caused more indignation against Tyndale among the clergy than his deliberate decision to avoid the words "priest," "church"

79

and "charity" in his translation. He preferred "seniors" or "elders," "congregation," and "love."

His reasons were sound. The Greek words for "church" and "charity" did not bear the meaning, or carry with them the associations, which the English words "church" and "charity" had come to have in the Catholic Church. Tyndale was defeated in this case, though the nineteenth-century Revised Version of the Bible accepted his view in one instance, substituting "love" for charity in I Cor. xiii.

There are no graphic incidents in the life of this plucky and combative little scholar, to whom, as much as to the committee who compiled the Authorized Version of the Bible in the reign of James I, we owe one of the glories of English literature. It does not appear that he ever had a personal interview with the burly and formidable Defender of the Faith, whom he never tried to flatter.

He was not in the position of Dean Colet of St. Paul's, who preached a strong pacifist sermon when the King was preparing to lead an army into France. "The King was in some apprehension lest the soldiers whom he was on the point of leading abroad should feel their courage gone through this discourse." So Henry sent for Colet, gave him lunch, and took him into his garden at Greenwich. He "wished the Dean to say at some other time, and with clearer explanation, what he had already said with perfect truth, that for Christians no war was a just one. And this was for the sake of the rough soldiers, who might put a different construction on his words from that which the Dean had intended." "Let every man have his own doctor," he said afterwards, "but this is the doctor for me." Henry, with all his faults, knew a man when he saw one.

There are few now who would agree with Chillingworth that "the Bible is the religion of Protestants." There are three principal seats of authority in religion—the Church, the Book and the Inner Light, which William James has taught us to call religious experience. To be complete, we ought to add Natural Law, the Words of the historical Jesus, Conscience and Reason; but for our purposes the Church, the Book and the Inner Light will suffice.

The Reformers needed an external authority to set against that of the Catholic Church, and found it in the Bible, which the Catholics also regarded as infallible, though they added that the Church alone had the right to determine the text and the interpretation. It was not till 1836, three centuries after Tyndale, that an English translation for Catholics was made from the Hebrew and Greek, instead of from the Vulgate.

The appeal from the authority of the Church to the Scriptures was anathematized in 787, and as late as 1824 a Papal encyclical deplored the

world-wide activity of the British and Foreign
Bible Society, which publishes the text only,
without comment, and called upon priests to safeguard their flocks from this deadly pest.

Bible societies were again condemned by the
Popes in 1844, 1846 and (grouped with Socialism
and Communism) in 1860. Heiler in 1921 found
that "the Scriptures are not widely read by the
Catholic laity."

But the authority of the Book has declined very
rapidly among Protestants. We cannot reproach the
Roman Catholics for not reading their Bibles, for
our own people have almost ceased to read them.
Just when, for the first time, it is possible to read the
Scriptures intelligently, with the help of a good
commentary, the habit of Bible reading has gone
out.

No sensible man wishes to revive the old superstitious belief in verbal inspiration, or the text-
slinging arguments which it produced. But no
Englishman is educated who does not know his
Bible. Thanks to William Tyndale as much as
anyone, it is an integral part of our national
tradition, one of the chief formative influences in
the British character.

In the sixteenth century, after "Bloody Mary's"
emissaries had burnt all the English Bibles they
could find, the Book became a precious possession,
a pledge of religious freedom. So it remained for
300 years, in all pious households.

The Christian family brought to their favourite religious exercise more than they found in the Book itself, parts of which, as we can all see now, are not of great value to the modern reader. But the Old Testament was read in the light of the New; it was allegorized and Christianized. A sacred book is worth, to us, what we can make of it.

The third of my three "seats of authority"—the Inner Light, or religious experience—is now more trusted than either Church or Book. But it is this inner light by which the Catholic idealizes his Church and the Protestant his Bible. Religion must twine itself round some support; it needs a point of attachment to the external world. And when we think of the spiritual treasures which we have found in the New Testament, let us not forget the brave man who gave his life to secure for his countrymen the precious privilege of reading it in our own tongue, the persecuted exile whose poor body was burnt to ashes in October, 1536.

April, 1939.

V

LIVES OF CHRIST

Sɪʀ Hᴀʟʟ Cᴀɪɴᴇ's *Life of Christ*, published, by his orders, only after a long interval, will be read with sympathetic interest by those who remember his great popularity as a novelist.

It is an immensely long book, containing over half a million words, and I fear it cannot be treated as a contribution to scholarship. But the author is revealed as an earnest Christian, who was willing to devote several years of his life to reading and meditating upon all that he could find about the central figure in human history.

I was once approached by an American publisher, whose name I shall certainly not reveal, with a request that I would write my autobiography. The terms were more than generous. When I refused, he asked me to write a life of Christ instead, for which he could not offer me quite so much money!

These modern Lives of Christ—they are all modern—are a very interesting phenomenon. The materials for a biography of the Founder of our religion are quite inadequate. The Gospels of Matthew, Mark and Luke were compiled for the use of the Churches towards the close of the first century. Their aim is partly devotional, partly for instruction, and partly apologetic. There was no

Boswell to take down the words of the Master as they fell from His lips, and we have undoubtedly lost much which we should value more than stories of miracles, in which the faith and love of the Church hoped to do honour to its Lord.

Nevertheless, I believe that the character of the human Christ, and the main features of His teaching, are truly depicted in these documents. We are told that "He was far above His reporters," and many of His sayings seem too great and wise not to be authentic.

The Fourth Gospel is an inspired interpretation of the Life of Christ in its eternal and universal significance; it is the work of an unknown Christian mystic who wrote between A.D. 100 and 120.

A few modern writers have argued that Christ is a mere "cult-hero," not a historical character at all. The great Harnack, when he was asked whether this theory was possible, replied, "No, it is certainly untenable; but perhaps only a scholar has the right to say so." The plain man may be content with this; no scholar of the first rank has any doubt that Jesus of Nazareth really lived.

But the mere fact that such a theory can be made plausible shows how unstable the historical foundations for a biography of Jesus are. No one who valued his reputation for sanity would write a book to prove that Cicero or Julius Cæsar never existed.

The same uncertainty is disclosed by the theory associated with the name of Schweitzer, that the historical Jesus was a deluded prophet whose message was that a supernatural cataclysm was about to bring the present world-order to an end. Since nothing of the kind happened, a man who went about frightening people in this way would be a very odd person to choose as a recipient of divine honours. The outcome of this theory is to separate sharply the Jesus of history from the Christ of the Church's worship. We acknowledge, as Loisy says, *"comme deux Christs."* The connection between them seems almost accidental. The historical Church, with its rather chequered career, is virtually put in the place of the shadowy figure of the Founder.

Personally, as I have already said, I think the Gospels give us a true picture of the human Christ, mixed, no doubt, with additions of secondary value. The divine life under human conditions is there once for all revealed. We have never got beyond that picture and we never shall.

Nevertheless, we do not worship a historical person whose part in human affairs was played nearly two thousand years ago. "We are converted to the Lord as Spirit," as a German commentator says. The Christ who is "with us always even to the end of the world," who "liveth in me," as St. Paul says, is a living Power, not a dead prophet and a doubtful memory.

During the greater part of Church history, Christians have been content with this spiritual communion, and have paid little attention to the details of the Galilean ministry, of which it seems that even St. Paul was content to know very little, though he never doubted the identity of "the Spirit of Jesus" with the crucified and risen prophet of Nazareth.

Now, however, we want to picture Jesus as He lived among men. We think of Him taking those long walks among the hills of Palestine, gay in early spring with scarlet anemones, more beautiful than Solomon in all his glory, pausing to point lessons from farming and husbandry, and sometimes joining in the social life of the country folk.

We also, without meaning it, modernize His character, and draw Him as what we consider the perfect man. Sometimes the itch for romance has led writers into irreverence and bad taste. Renan's *Life of Jesus* is like a French novel. His hero is not above pretending to work miracles, and at Gethsemane He may have been thinking of the girls "who might have consented to love Him!"

Sir Hall Caine suggests that Judas was in love with Mary Magdalene, and betrayed his Master out of jealousy!

Dean Farrar's sentimentality is less mawkish, but cloying. "Very little," said a schoolboy, "is said about this in the Gospels, but there is a full description in Farrar's *Life of Christ*."

Other biographers are more interested in our Lord's teaching, and they are tempted to find in it what they would like Him to have taught. A

German speaks of His "frank manliness and power, with both feet planted firmly on the earth." Socialists have described Him as "*le bon sans-culotte.*" Seeley's *Ecce Homo* depicts a model Englishman; an American has drawn an unmistakable Yankee.

We need not be contemptuous of this tendency. Christ really speaks to every true man in his own language. It is the heavenly Christ no doubt, who so speaks; but there has been a real incarnation, and not merely a diffused revival of spiritual religion.

If these very unscientific and uncritical "Lives" help us to know and love our Master better, we ought not to be severe with their authors. The important question is, "What does Jesus mean to me?" It is not profitable to seek the living among the dead.

History, even when it is better documented than our record of the life of Christ can ever be, is not the key which unlocks every door. "Slowly the Bible of the race is writ." "I have yet many things to say unto you, but ye cannot bear them now." "The Spirit of Jesus" is still among us.

October, 1938.

VI

AWAY FROM IT ALL

TRAVELLERS in Egypt who have left the Nile Valley
to camp out for a few days in the desert, or in South
Africa have made long journeys over the lonely
veldt, generally agree that they have had a spiritual
experience which they would not willingly have
missed. They talk of the pure air and the wide
prospects; but the real attraction is the sense of
loneliness and emptiness.

The jungle, where man is crowded out by swarming life, hostile or indifferent, is a thing of horror;
but in the desert a man feels alone with God. The
sea gives us something of the same feeling—"the
moving waters at their priestlike task," as Keats
says.

The religion of the desert is bare and a little
inhuman. It allows no half-tones, only black and
white; no intermediaries between God and man;
no artistic representations of the divine; no genial
"idolatry," so natural to the rest of mankind. The
descendants of the pastoral nomads rejected Hellenized and Romanized Christianity, and reverted
to a religion more congenial to them, a religion in
which the divine omnipotence blazes in solitary
splendour, like the sun over the desert.

One of the strangest aberrations in the whole of

human history is the voluntary flight of many thousands of men and women from civilized life to the African desert, where they often underwent privations and sometimes self-inflicted cruelties, such as the harshest government would hardly impose upon the lowest criminals or political prisoners. Miss Helen Waddell's *The Desert Fathers* has revived the interest of many readers in this chapter of early Christianity. There was a violent epidemic of flight from the world, which aroused dismay and anger in the society of the later Roman Empire.

In reality, Simeon Stylites on his pillar, the Dendrites, who lived in trees, the Bosci, who lived on grass, like Nebuchadnezzar, and the Catenati, who loaded themselves with chains, were not typical hermits. There was a certain emulation in austerities, as there is to-day among the fakirs of India, but the majority did not torment themselves.

Even now there are many who choose to live in solitude, not always from religious motives: and I know of one Anglican "anchoress" who has walled herself up in a churchyard. There used to be many such who never left their cells, but they were allowed to gossip from the window. "Be not cackling anchoresses," says a fourteenth-century manual.

The motives for wishing to be a hermit are various. We have no right to say that a life of prayer and contemplation is wasted. Even from the most materialistic point of view, the ascetic, if he produces nothing, consumes next to nothing. He is not a serious burden on the community.

No doubt there are some who think they are attracted by God when they are only repelled by men. Those who are not religious keep cats.

Apart from the ambition to be a "spiritual athlete"—a phrase which they often used—or a mystic who by travelling through strange seas of thought alone arrives at last at the beatific vision, there may be other motives for flight from human society.

We all have to settle our accounts with our surroundings as best we may. Hegel says that a man who has work which suits him and a wife whom he loves has squared his accounts with life. But most of us have troubles and anxieties at one time or another. How do we try to protect ourselves?

We may raise a fraction to unity either by increasing the numerator or by diminishing the denominator. One method or the other, or both together, we all try.

Ambition is an attempt to satisfy our demands upon life. It is not inevitably self-defeating, like the direct pursuit of pleasure, and when success comes, it usually, but not always, brings some happiness. But I think most successful men admit that the struggle was the prize, and that the prize in itself was hardly worth all that had to be done, and renounced, to win it.

In some states of society, for a short time only,

the rewards of industry and ability are so great, and within the reach of so many, that "success" is almost deified and is worshipped by all. So it used to be in the United States; but even there it is ceasing to be so. In Europe, this kind of individual ambition is plainly out of reach except for a few.

Another ideal has taken its place on the Continent, that of merging oneself in a group, with nothing to hope and nothing to fear. The idealistic element is supplied by power politics. The German and the Italian know that they are badly off, but all are in the same boat, and at the back of their minds is the belief that the low-standard nations will in the long run win against the high-standard nations like England and America. So they are content to be automata in the service of the totalitarian State. It is not a very high ideal, but it seems at present to make them happy.

The other time-honoured solution is to diminish our wants. Such is the wisdom of Buddha, the Stoics, the Puritans and Schopenhauer. Abolish desire, and you are invulnerable.

True Christianity does not offer to make us invulnerable, but almost all the philosophies do; and this is one of the chief motives of flight from the world.

But though we may run away from our friends and our duties, we cannot run away from ourselves, or, as they would have put it in those days, we cannot run away from the devil.

We understand better now that the forcible repression of all our natural instincts is a mistake. This is so well known that it is hardly worth repeating, and the deserts are likely to remain uninhabited.

An occasional retirement to some Robinson Crusoe's island might be good for many of us. St. Cuthbert used to bolt from his diocese and hide himself on the Farne Islands for prayer and meditation. It is possible that some of our bishops might improve their sermons by this method.

There are also times when even the happiest family man murmurs the words of a well-known hymn, "Peace, perfect peace, with loved ones far away."

August, 1938.

VII

MAKING THE CLERGY CHEAPJACKS

A PROMINENT Church layman, whose orthodoxy
has the stiffness of a poker and its occasional
warmth, has come forward again with the old
accusation that the Liberal clergy are dishonest
men who fall short of the standard of honour which
is accepted by respectable laymen.

The clergy, according to this view, are paid
advocates who have to speak to their brief. Their
brief is to defend the literal and scientific truth of
certain dogmatic formulas which were drawn up
some 1,500 or 1,600 years ago. These documents
are authoritative for all future time. They cannot
be revised or altered except by a General Council of
the Church, and since there are several independent
Churches, such a Council can never meet.

It is as if no Act of Parliament were valid unless it
were passed at a joint session of the House of
Commons and the American Congress. The Church,
therefore, can never escape from the tyranny of the
dead hand.

The charge of dishonesty is offensive and unjust.
What possible motive can a man have for opposing
the tradition of the elders except the conviction that
it is better to suffer for speaking the truth than that
the truth should suffer for want of our speaking?

94

For he has to suffer. It is not pleasant to be abused and hated as a heretic, not only by simple old-fashioned people but by truculent and furious fanatics. It is easy enough to escape this kind of trouble by merely holding our tongues. A man who can hold his tongue can hold anything, even a bishopric. But some of us remember the saying of Tertullian, about A.D. 200: "Our Lord called Himself the Truth, not Tradition."

One thing is quite certain. As Erasmus said, "By identifying the new learning with heresy, you are making orthodoxy synonymous with ignorance." Complaints are made that men of first-class ability are scarce in the Church. Well, the bishops have only the laity to choose from; but if we are bound hand and foot by obsolete tradition, they will not even get men of high character. They will get only dunces, liars and bigots.

Has orthodoxy really stood still ever since the first century? Very far from it. Even in the New Testament we can trace the growth of doctrine about the Person of Christ. It begins with apotheosis and ends with incarnation.

St. Paul, when he brought the Gospel into Europe, took the boldest step in the whole history of the Church. He introduced Christianity into the orbit of Greek and Roman civilization, thereby winning Europe and losing Asia.

In the following centuries the Church carried off into its hive the treasures of Greek philosophy, at

95

first Plato and the Stoics, and later, with the Mediæval schoolmen, Aristotle. In the fourth century, and again in the thirteenth, the Church was fully abreast of the science and philosophy of the day. Augustine and Thomas Aquinas were the ablest men of their times.

Then came the Renaissance, and the almost simultaneous discoveries of the world beyond the seas, the universe over our heads, and the treasures of classical antiquity. Great readjustments of theology were required. But just then churchmen were so busy burning each other and cutting each other's throats that very little was done. So began the "conflict between religion and science" of which we heard so much in the last century. It was a real conflict; but though the Church made many concessions, the leeway which began centuries before was never made up.

Still, the change within my own lifetime has been enormous, and we owe it all to brave men who were not afraid to oppose tradition in the name of truth.

I can remember the time when a Christian was expected to believe that the world was created only 4,000 years before Christ; that every word in the Bible was historical fact; that heaven was a place above our heads, and many other things which only American fundamentalists at Dayton, Tennessee, and similar places, believe now. All this lumber has been swept away during my lifetime.

If it had not been swept away, it would be difficult for any educated man to be a Christian.

We live in an age dominated by natural science. Even if we do not know much science ourselves, we think of the world as a realm of law. The old arguments from miracle and prophecy do not appeal to us at all. We can appreciate the warning of Christ: "Except ye see signs and wonders, ye will not believe."

We do not want to see signs and wonders, and we are beginning to realize that miracles, taken as flat historical recitals, prove nothing that is of interest to religion. We do not need them. Our belief in the divinity of Christ rests on other foundations.

I have sometimes spoken of historical dogmas as bridges between the seen and the unseen, between the world of facts and the world of values. They are not the foundation of faith, but with very many persons they are created by faith, and are believed as congruous with faith. For the majority of Christians they have a sacramental value. The Greek Fathers spoke of them as "mysteries," the Greek word for sacraments. Those who prize them for what they symbolize quite rightly refuse to give them up. We do not wish them to give them up.

But a large and perhaps increasing number of men and women do not find it natural to think in this way. They are firmly convinced of the divinity of Christ, but they do not feel that the doctrines of the virgin birth and the ascension into heaven follow necessarily from this belief. They do not wish to deny these dogmas, but they claim to be allowed to relegate them to the sphere of pious opinions which are not integral parts of their living faith.

I do not claim unlimited freedom for the clergy. Many years ago I had the curious experience of receiving almost on the same day two copies of a set of sermons by an unorthodox priest, one from his bishop, who wished to unfrock him, the other from a society which at that time was protecting the victims of heresy hunts. After reading the sermons I advised the society not to take up the case; I thought the bishop was quite right. But this was a man who seemed to believe hardly anything; he had clearly mistaken his profession.

It is a very different thing when a devout Christian is stigmatized as dishonourable because he cannot accept in the literal sense such articles in the Creeds as those which affirm the "descent into hell," the "ascension into heaven," and the "resurrection of the flesh."

What I think we ought to hope for is that a time may come when a Christian will not be asked to do violence to his intellectual conscience. The demands of Christianity are severe enough, but they do not include what is sometimes called the sacrifice of the intellect. There have been times, as I have said, when the best philosophy and science of the day were Christian.

Why should not this happen again? But it never

can happen if the laity insist on the clergy being cheapjacks paid to cry up certain wares, whether they are true or not. That is the way to bring the Church into deserved contempt.

There is such a thing as progressive revelation, and what science has taught us about the laws of Nature is, for the religious mind, a revelation of the will and character of the Creator.

February, 1939.

VIII

A NEW REFORMATION

I HAVE been reading a new book by Professor Angus of Sydney University called *Essential Christianity*, and find much in it with which I cordially agree. It is a plea for a new Reformation, the kind of Reformation which Erasmus would have welcomed, but which was quite impossible in the days of Luther, Calvin and Henry VIII.

I agree with Professor Angus in wishing for it; whether it is likely to happen is another question. Most of those who support the Churches are fairly well content with things as they are. Most of those who do not are not interested. Are there enough who are both interested and dissatisfied, to carry out a reform on a large scale? I doubt it, though the future of organized Christianity may be at stake.

Canon F. R. Barry, who believes in plain speaking as I do, has said that "the one really formidable argument against the truth of the Christian religion is the record of the Christian Church." Non-Christians have said the same thing. "These Christians," said Nietzsche, "must show that they have been redeemed before I can believe in their Redeemer." And again: "There has been only one

Christian; He died upon the Cross." Swinburne, with his habitual intemperance of language, said, "I could believe in the Crucified if he came to me without his leprous bride the Church."

I have ventured to say myself that every human institution, even the Church, ends by strangling the ideas which it was founded to protect. I might add that when the devil captures an institution which was formed to defeat him, he never changes the label.

This is one side of the case. The other is that there has been a real apostolical succession in the lives of true Christians, and that such lives are the best proof of the truth of their belief. There is no refutation of a holy life.

It is an old quarrel—the choice between institutionalism and mysticism, between the religion of authority and the religion of the Spirit. The two tendencies are both very apparent in the religious thought of our day. On one side there has been an increased tendency to rely on authority, whether the authority chosen be that of the Roman Church or the neo-Calvinist fundamentalism of Karl Barth.

Certainly, if authority A tells me to believe, and authority B tells me not to believe, and I decide to follow authority A without examining the evidence, that is much the same as saying that I believe because I choose, which is not a very dignified attitude for a rational man. But many find it an immense relief to give up worrying, and to follow a guide who has imposing credentials.

On the other hand, the argument from what, since William James, has been called religious experience, and in earlier times was called the testimony of the Holy Spirit or the inner light, now holds the central place in the defence of the faith. It is the primary evidence for the truth of religion; it is not endangered by the collapse of the old arguments from miracle and prophecy, which have fared badly against the assaults of natural science and historical criticism. It enables the believer to stand on his own feet.

A commanded faith is no faith at all. An unexamined life, as Plato said, is not worth living.

Institutionalism is totalitarianism in religion. Hitler dislikes and persecutes the Roman Church because it is a rival corporation of the same kind as his own dictatorship. There is no room for two God-States in the same country. Until the appearance of the new dictatorships, the Papacy was the sole survivor of the absolute type of State.

The laws of the theocratic State are dogmas, theological propositions promulgated by authority. They are responsible for our unhappy divisions, just as dictatorships promote international strife. Devotion unites; theology divides. Christendom has never been divided in the chambers where good men pray; but the *odium theologicum* is a proverb.

The religion of the Spirit can tolerate and even welcome unity without uniformity; theology cannot. The war-cry of institutionalism is "Outside the Church there is no salvation"—the Church being one particular Church. This is perhaps the most un-Christian slogan ever uttered. It has drenched Europe with blood, and poisoned men's minds with fanatical hatred.

I am not one of those who think that any stigma is good enough to beat a dogma. A dogma is only an authoritative decision terminating a debate. Opinions are fluid until the authorities think it time to close the discussion. Sometimes they are right. It would have been useless to prolong the hair-splitting debates about the Person of Christ which the Byzantines and Alexandrians found so interesting. But dogma is congealed, petrified, crystallized doctrine. It may have been the correct answer to the problems which had divided theologians, but the human mind does not stand still. As Froude said: "If medicine had been regulated three hundred years ago by Act of Parliament; if there had been Thirty-nine Articles of Physic, and every licensed practitioner had been compelled under pains and penalties to compound his drugs by the prescriptions of Henry the Eighth's physician, Dr. Butt, it is easy to conjecture in what state of health the people of this country would at present be found."

The case is even stronger against fixed theological forms, for the ingredients of drugs retain their properties, but words change their meaning insensibly. For instance, the Greek Fathers used the word *theos* where we should hesitate to use the word God, and the word *person* in theology has a very different meaning from what the law calls a person, a subject of rights, duties and liabilities.

The main objection to dogmas is that since they are pronounced to be absolutely true, it is very difficult to alter them.

The Roman Church in the last century made two new dogmas: the Immaculate Conception and the Infallibility of the Pope. It is possible to remove books from the index of prohibited books; since 1835 (not earlier !) Catholics have been allowed to believe that the earth moves round the sun.

Professor Angus argues that the original Gospel was a layman's religion, appealing to the individual conscience and intelligence. Christ came to make men spiritually free; but, as St. Paul found, many people prefer bondage. And before long the Church stooped to conquer, to command rather than to lead, to dictate rather than to inspire, to set up a code rather than to teach men to use their own consciences and to walk by the Spirit. The priest ousted the prophet; the Church stepped into the place of the indwelling Spirit of Christ.

Therefore, we need a new Reformation. The first Reformation divided Christendom; the next Reformation ought to unite all real Christians, while accepting diversities of worship and belief. So

A NEW REFORMATION

"Christianity may once more become what it was in the beginning, the rallying centre for heroic souls." For, as Principal Jacks says, "Religion is a power which develops the hero in the man at the expense of the coward in the man."

March, 1939.

105

IX

CATHOLIC MODERNISM

I HAVE been reading a most interesting and delightful book of reminiscences. It is *My Way of Faith*, by Miss Maude Petre.

The Roman Catholics in England divide the members of their Church into "old Catholics" and "converts." The typical "old Catholic" is not bitter or unfair. He is intensely proud, in a well-bred way. To belong to a Church which (as he would say) has been in existence for only 400 years would be an insult to his coat of arms and the family ghost.

He employs a priest to look after his soul just as he employs a lawyer to manage his affairs and a doctor to keep him in health. He believes that the priest is honest, and presumably knows his business. For a layman to study controversial theology in order to test the qualifications of his spiritual adviser is as unnecessary as to study law in order to satisfy himself of the skill of his solicitor, or medicine in order to make sure of his doctor.

Miss Petre belongs to one of these aristocratic families. She records a characteristic remark of her father: "Why should I repeat my vows to God? He knows, I suppose, that He can trust the word of a gentleman !" Her description of her first home, in one of those enormous and, of course, unrestricted families which are characteristic of the "old Catholics," is delightful. How well I can sympathize with the children's detestation of the milk puddings —rice, sago, tapioca—with which the Victorian parents "subdued the pride of sinful flesh" in their offspring !

She tells us of her long hesitation in making the decision which has to be made by every Catholic girl of good family—whether to marry, and perhaps have the coveted privilege of being the mother of priests and nuns, or to enter a sisterhood. She chose the latter, and as might have been expected in her case—for she was not only of noble birth, but a woman of great ability and force of character— soon became head of her community. In middle life she returned to "the world," but was no doubt still pledged to a single life.

The chief personal interest in her book is the account of her ardent Platonic friendship with Father George Tyrrell, which she relates with the proud candour of a great lady who knows that she need not fear being misunderstood. It was this friendship which brought her into the Catholic Modernist movement, and it was her loyalty to the memory of Tyrrell which after his death led to her collision with the authorities of her Church. This movement, which was eventually crushed or driven underground by the iron hand of authority, is one of the most interesting chapters in the religious history of our time.

The two chief representatives of Modernism in this country were Baron Friedrich von Hügel and George Tyrrell. The Baron, the son of a distinguished diplomat by a Scotch mother, was the foremost theologian of his time in England. A man of immense learning, he devoted himself chiefly to the study of Christian mysticism, a subject which requires a comprehensive knowledge of philosophy.

When I am asked by a thoughtful agnostic to recommend a book which sets forth the Christian position with convincing intellectual power, I advise him to read von Hügel's *Eternal Life*. This book was intended for an article in Hastings's *Encyclopædia of Religion and Ethics*: but when the Baron sent in 400 pages, the Editor was reluctantly obliged to reject it as being somewhat out of scale.

Von Hügel was acutely conscious that some of the traditional doctrines of the Church were fatally undermined by modern science and historical criticism, and he thought for a time that the philosophy of Bergson, and the theology of the French Modernists, who had already founded a school, opened a way to a new conception of truth in religion, which might set the dogmas of the Church above high-water mark.

Surprise was often expressed that the authorities at Rome left him undisturbed, when they were coming down so heavily on other Modernists. But that astute body seldom makes mistakes. Von Hügel was a layman, and a very valuable asset to their Church.

He was a saint, and so able a thinker that he had great influence over Anglican scholars. He was also not of the stuff out of which martyrs are made. He would never defy authority. Moreover, though he was not the man to own himself in the wrong, he probably came to realize that he was on a very dangerous path; how dangerous it was I hope to show presently.

In consequence, he ceased to lead the Modernists, and remained a great Christian philosopher, mistrusted only by some of his own communion. Many Catholics shake their heads over him, and call him "the man who ruined George Tyrrell."

Tyrrell was a wild Irishman, who came under the influence of von Hügel, and followed the Modernist path with a fearless logic quite alien to the temperament of the cautious German. His friends hung on to his coat-tails and begged him to be careful, but his Irish blood was up, and nothing could restrain him from throwing down his gauntlet in the face of a Society which never forgives disobedience.

He was first expelled from the Society of Jesus, and then excommunicated. The unrelenting Church condemned him to be buried like a dog; and when his friend, the Abbé Bremond, read the service over his body, he himself fell into disgrace, and only escaped excommunication by signing an abject repudiation of Modernism.

Tyrrell's books are brilliantly written, and are (or were) read with admiration by many who never realized how far he had departed from traditional orthodoxy; but he underestimated the penetration of his critics, and when a private letter, in which he gave himself away badly, fell into the hands of the authorities, his doom was sealed.

Miss Petre confesses that her early ambition was to be a philosopher, a saint and a martyr. To a great extent she has attained the third of her aspirations. She now finds herself "in a position of solitude and abandonment"; her co-religionists cannot forget that she was closely connected with a movement which was condemned by the Pope as "a compendium of all the heresies," and which they believe to be now dead.

But apart from her great loyalty to her friend, I doubt whether she is or ever was really a Modernist. She resented having every independent thought squashed by authority; she hated the doctrine of eternal torment; but her philosophy was not deep enough for her to realize that Modernism rests upon the deep current of anti-intellectualism which has swept modern philosophy quite away from its old moorings.

She calls herself a Platonist, and cannot understand why her friend Laberthonnière hated St.

Thomas Aquinas. But the new philosophy has no use either for Plato or for St. Thomas; it is fundamentally antipathetic to what Catholics call the perennial philosophy, the system of thought which underlies the whole of Christian theology. This has, I think, become clearer since the Modernist controversy; it does not diminish the tragedy which ruined a number of earnest men whose only wish was to place Catholic doctrine on a sounder foundation.

My own connection with the Catholic Modernist movement began with a furious sermon which I preached against it before the University of Oxford. I did not fully realize then that it was part of a much larger movement. I should not have liked it any better if I had.

April, 1939.

X

THE BUCHMAN GROUP CONTROVERSY

FOR some unexplained reason, the name of Oxford has always had a greater publicity value than that of Cambridge. A Fellow of a Cambridge college once said to me: "The reason is that we do not educate our young men *down* to writing in newspapers"—a nasty one for me. There can be no doubt of the fact; Oxford is always in the limelight; the Cam is a very quiet river.

The original Oxford Movement, or Anglo-Catholic revival, really did begin in Oxford. Its leaders, Newman, Pusey, Keble, Hurrell Froude and others, were all resident in the University, or closely connected with it. Later developments, such as ritualism and Christian Socialism, partly altered its character. I have ventured to call modern Anglo-Catholicism the London, Brighton and South Coast religion; but it has never lost its connection with Oxford.

We have also heard of the Oxford manner, and we know what that means. Chaucer had already noticed it. "Souninge [sounding] in moral vertu was his speche, and gladly wolde he learn and gladly teche." "He is not as other men are," says J. R. Green; "he has a deep, quiet contempt for other men. Oxford is his home; and beyond Oxford

112

lie only waste regions of shallowness and inaccuracy."

"They entered the world," says Samuel Johnson, "prepared to show wisdom by their discourse, and moderation by their silence; to instruct the modest with easy gentleness, and repress the ostentatious by seasonable superciliousness." "I can't myself make out," Cardinal Newman wrote, "why an Oxford man should be known from another. It is a fearful thing that we, as it were, exhale ourselves with every breath we draw."

It is not for me to say whether these strictures are justified or not. Probably the Oxford man is sometimes (as was said in a skit on a very distinguished son of Eton and Balliol), "a most superior person"; but I have met supercilious people who had received such education as they had elsewhere.

Then there is the so-called Oxford accent. Sometimes this is merely the way of speaking English which is common to all gentlefolk in England at the present time. As this is a social shibboleth, it is resented; some people might prefer the modified Cockney (e.g. "gyme" for "game"), which was fashionable with young ladies thirty years ago. But sometimes it means the slipshod pronunciation of unaccented syllables, which is certainly too common.

I remember Du Maurier's picture of a young exquisite declaiming to his admirers: "Glad lady mine, who glittahest with a shimmah of summah athwart the lawn, Can'st tell me which is bittahest, the glammah of eve or the glimmah of dawn? Like a buttahfly dost thou fluttah by, O whence and O whither art come and gawn?"

Is this accent commoner at Oxford than at other places where people of the same class congregate? I do not think so. At any rate, Oxford is now so cosmopolitan and so democratic that you may hear every kind of accent spoken there—Aberdeen, Lancashire, New York, Sydney, Calcutta, and what not.

An active controversy is now going on about the claim of Mr. Buchman's Group Movement to be registered under the name of Oxford. Surely there cannot be the slightest doubt that Mr. A. P. Herbert, one of the representatives of Oxford University in Parliament, is entirely justified in objecting.

The movement neither has nor ever has had any connection with Oxford. It is a typically American religious revival, like Mrs. Eddy's Christian Science, and the Gospel according to Moody and Sankey, or Torrey and Alexander. Its methods of propaganda and publicity are emphatically transatlantic. Nothing more alien to the spirit of Oxford can be imagined. Its present headquarters are in London.

The letters of those who support Mr. Herbert make it quite clear that the word "Oxford" was chosen by the leaders of the movement because of its publicity value, and that the imaginary connection with the University is exploited as part of its propaganda. Surely this is not honest; and now that the claim has been so fully investigated, it will probably do the movement more harm than good to continue to make it. Why cannot Mr. Buchman overcome his natural modesty and call his creation after his own name? Methodism is not ashamed of John Wesley, nor Jesuitism of Ignatius of Loyola.

The suggestions on the other side, that "Oxford" is merely a trade name with no significance, are disingenuous. "Windsor Soap" is not meant to imply that the Royal Family "use no other." The "Gladstone Bag" was not intended to deter good Conservatives from taking these suitcases for their week-ends. The vendors of "the Pickwick, the Owl, and the Waverley Pen" advertised their commodities as "a boon and a blessing to men"; they did not promise that those who used them would become novelists.

Oxford men do not wish their university to be associated with Mr. Buchman's movement, because they know that in this case Oxford is not, and is not intended to be, merely a trade name.

In joining this protest, I am acting in what I believe to be the best interests of the movement. It is a religious movement, and therefore its methods ought to be above suspicion. Those who think to establish a great revival of Christianity by ways so painfully unlike the manner of the great religious leaders are building their house upon the sand. It may win popularity and apparent success for a time, but it will not last. In Oxford itself it is said to be losing ground rapidly.

I will give no opinion as to the value of the Group movement. I cannot say that I like what I have heard of their methods, but they seem to have brought many young people back to Christianity, which, I fear, is more than most of us, the ordained clergy, can say. The well-known advice of Gamaliel, to "let these men alone, lest we be found even to fight against God," is never out of date.

The young people have lost confidence in their elders, who allowed the world to drift into a ruinous war and seem capable of allowing it to drift into another, still more ruinous. The young people think for themselves, and many of them have hopes in this new movement. I will not say a word to discourage them. But unless the strategy of Mr. Buchman and his friends is quite above-board, there will be a disillusionment which will sweep away all the good that has been done.

One lesson which, I think, the Churches may learn is that if we want to put new life into our Christianity, we must give the lay folk something to do. The Church of England has not been very successful in this way. To come to church once a week is not enough to hold a religious community together, and before long they cease even to come to church once a week.

Possibly, but I am not sure, it may be a good

thing to break down the reserve in which the average Englishman hides his deepest convictions. At least, he says that they are his deepest; but they are sometimes so deep that they never show at all, and we cannot always be sure that they are there. At any rate, many young people feel they want to "share" their convictions and their difficulties. Their confidences create a bond of sympathy, and they criticize each other, sometimes wisely, no doubt.

I hope that those who think that they owe much to Mr. Buchman will not think that these remarks have been conceived in any spirit of hostility; it is not so.

June, 1939.

XI

ARE WE CHRISTIANS?

AMONG my predecessors in the Deanery of St. Paul's during the last century, the most distinguished, the wisest and best, was R. W. Church. In one of his best-known books, *The Gifts of Civilization*, I find the following passage:

"It seems impossible to conceive three things more opposite at first sight to the Sermon on the Mount than War, Law and Trade; yet Christian society has long since made up its mind about them, and we all accept them as among the necessities or occupations of human society. Christ has in many ways transformed that society, which is only for this time and life. . . . Even war and riches, even the high places of earthly honour have been touched by His spirit, have found how to be Christian."

Considering who the author of these words was, I know of no more startling illustration of the change from Victorian complacency and optimism to the discontent, the pessimism, the unquiet conscience of our own day. Is modern society effectively Christian? Is big business Christian? Can we accept war as "a necessary occupation" of Christian nations?

And how odd it seems to call the State "Law," as if it were a mere policeman, whereas the modern

State is becoming more and more like the Leviathan of Hobbes, a universal and jealous tyrant, claiming control over all that we do, and in most countries over all that we say or think.

There are three questions which have to be answered: (1) Are our institutions compatible with Christianity? (2) If they are, are they worked in a Christian spirit? (3) If they are not, does that mean that Christianity is a failure?

(1) On this point the traditional teaching of the Church is fairly clear. Accepting from the Stoics the idea of a Law of Nature, which is eternal and irrevocable, and above all positive law, so that human laws which contravene it ought not to be obeyed, the Church distinguished between the absolute Law of Nature, which might be observed if human nature were perfect, and the relative Law of Nature, which is binding upon us in our present condition, though beatified spirits will know nothing of it.

The relative Law of Nature sanctions private property, law and punishment, and (as Dean Church says) war. Later civil codes, such as the American constitution, say that men have a natural right to life, liberty and happiness. The right to private property is included among natural rights, but not, I think, the right of bequest.

But all these rights, even the right to life, may be forfeited by misconduct. Private property is not sacred unless it is honestly acquired and decently used. The limits of the right of the State to tax property for public services and for national defence are left undetermined; but Communism has always been condemned, except by a few heretical sectaries.

The doctrine of the Law of Nature is necessary if we are to have any protection against the tyranny of the State, whether the State is an autocrat or a parliamentary majority. The Government has no absolute claim on our obedience, and it is in no sense a creator of right and wrong. But the limits of Natural Law are left vague, and are made more doubtful because the "Law of Christ" is super-imposed upon Natural Law, not contradicting but interpreting it. And the Law of Christ is the Law of Love. This may be held to mean that if Dives has no pity on Lazarus he is not fulfilling the conditions under which he may do what he will with his own.

Many of us however refuse to admit that war is justified by the relative Law of Nature. It may once have been a "necessary occupation" of mankind; it is so no longer; it is an anachronism and a gigantic folly. Unfortunately, we seem to be almost alone among European nations in holding this view.

With this exception, there is nothing incompatible with Christianity in our present institutions.

(2) Are they worked in a Christian spirit? They are not, and they never have been, but the sins of

society have not always been the same. The nine-teenth century gave a sort of religious character to movements that in themselves are neither ideal nor spiritual. Democracy swelled itself with hot air till it has burst like the frog in the fable. Patriotism has become insane nationalism. Economics have ab-sorbed all other ideal interests, so that even religion has been violently secularized.

The great task of Christianity, we are told, is to "abolish poverty." This is not much like the Sermon on the Mount. The real opinion of Christ on economics is that they are not worth bothering about. "Take no thought for your life, what ye shall eat or drink or wear." We cannot follow this precept literally; but it remains true that a secular-ized Christianity has neither savour nor salt. How many well-meaning persons have plunged into "the social question" hoping to find idealism and sacrifice, and have found only materialism and politicians !

Nevertheless, the paradox of Christianity is that while it demonetizes the world's currency very thoroughly, it is not otherworldly in dealing with human suffering. It never tells the sufferer that pain is imaginary, like Christian Science, or that we can conquer it by saying, "I don't care," like the Stoics. The Christian ought not to be indifferent to social reform. It is possible to spiritualize our religion overmuch, and sadly easy to think we are disinterested when we are only uninterested.

(3) If our society is not effectively Christian, does that mean that Christianity is a failure? We are so democratized that we are absurdly afraid of being in a minority. We have heard that broad is the way that leadeth to destruction, and many there be that go in thereat; but we are discouraged if we find ourselves in a half-empty church.

I know some popular churches which would be much emptier if the Gospel was preached in them. "Woe unto you when all men shall speak well of you, for so did the fathers of the false prophets." There is nothing which Christ impressed upon His disciples more insistently than that "the world" would always be against them.

The moral of Victorian optimism is that pride goeth before a fall; we have had a very nasty fall, and are not likely to forget it. Only for heaven's sake let the clergy, when they are in the pulpit, keep out of politics, and not suppose that Christianity offers a short cut to "a good time all round." There are no "Christian politics and economics"; there is only a Christian standard of values, and a Christian law of love.

July, 1939.

ENGLAND

I

LET US REMEMBER

AFTER twenty years we do not want to read articles or hear speeches or sermons about the armistice. We just want to pause and remember, and, I think, to remember in silence. Those two minutes are what we want, and for most of us they are enough.

They give us time to think of all the young lives, on both sides, cut short in those terrible four years. In many places there is a little service round the war-memorial which commemorates the men of the parish who gave their lives for their country. And speaking of war memorials, I never read a better inscription than that in the market-place of our post town, Wallingford:

> Pass not this stone in sorrow but in pride,
> And strive to live as nobly as they died.

After the little service on the steps of St. Paul's, I think my first thought, while I lived there, was of the long pageant of English history, continuous from Tudor times and earlier to our own perplexed and troubled lives. Famous passages of patriotic poetry began to run in my head.

I thought of the day when news came that the Spanish Armada had been sighted, and of

Macaulay's magnificent poem—yes, my sneering criticasters, it is a magnificent poem—beginning, "Attend, all ye who list to hear our noble England's praise." I thought of the picturesque processions of good Queen Bess, attended by her nobles splendid in cloak, doublet and hose. I thought of Shakespeare in his theatre, and the grand speeches in praise of England, of which I think John of Gaunt's in *Richard the Second* is the best. (The Agincourt speech in *Henry the Fifth* was recommended by the Germans as good war poetry; and so it is; but it is too flamboyant and bombastic, as Shakespeare must have known very well. He wrote it for the average playgoer.)

Then I followed the course of history to Puritan London, rather grim and grave. But Milton's patriotism, stern and lofty, was as genuine as Shakespeare's, and Andrew Marvell's famous "Ode to Cromwell," is noble poetry, whatever we may think of the sentiments.

Then Fleet Street and Cheapside saw the merry monarch and Samuel Pepys, who calls Gracechurch Street Gracious Street and Marylebone Marrowbone (pronunciation was more slipshod then even than now); till we come to the Great Fire, which destroyed one of the most beautiful, and most insanitary, cities in Europe.

Sir Christopher Wren soon rebuilt the Cathedral, but was not allowed to lay out the City in a cartwheel with converging spokes, like Washington.

So my thoughts passed on to the eighteenth century, the age of wits and coffee-houses and Dr. Johnson, who thought that a man who was tired of London must be tired of life; and thence to the long wars with Napoleon. These produced some splendid sonnets by Wordsworth, which were read with delight by our troops in France; some rebellious poetry by Shelley and Byron; some rather poor verse by Southey; and the novels of Jane Austen, who seems not to have been aware that her country was at war. Wellington is worthily commemorated by Tennyson, though I suspect that the real Wellington was an even greater general and not quite such a moral hero as some of his biographers describe him.

After Waterloo came the 100 years of peace, broken only by wars which never threatened our island peace and security, the golden age of our nation, as history will certainly call it. The old Queen, who as a girl promised to be a frisky Hanoverian, lived to represent her age, in its strength and limitations, perfectly. "When I know what the Queen thinks," said that fine aristocrat Lord Salisbury, "I know how the matter will appear to the great middle class!"

When I dreamed of the past in this way, George V, one of the very best of our kings, was still alive. He was a great patriot, and anything rather than a jingo. There is a legend that his last words were, "How's the Empire?" But I am told that he really murmured, "How's that, umpire?" a much more likely remark for an Englishman on his way to the Elysian Fields.

The nineteenth century culminated in the Diamond Jubilee, which I watched from the west parapet of St. Paul's. I thought I saw the little old lady watching mischievously the Lord Mayor mounting a horse with an unaccustomed cloak and sword. But nothing happened.

I had an uncomfortable feeling that the imperialistic swagger of that day was the pride that goeth before a fall. "And Nebuchadnezzar said, 'Is not this great Babylon that I have builded?'" Rudyard Kipling, as we remember, put this thought, which was in many minds, into fine poetry. Nemesis soon overtook us in the Boer War, and we have been in a chastened mood ever since.

The Great War produced a little poetry quite of the first rank. Rupert Brooke, Julian Grenfell and Wilfred Owen wrote poems which will never be forgotten. But nothing was written in the bombastic vein of Shakespeare and Marvell and Thomas Campbell, who exulted in the discomfiture of "all the might of Denmark's crown." Siegfried Sassoon and others displayed a mood of bitter disillusionment. No; the old exultation over scenes of slaughter is past, I hope for ever. Our troops never fought better, but they detested the whole business, and did not detest the enemy.

We might do worse than read first-hand

descriptions of acts of chivalry on both sides, such as those collected by Arthur Stanley in his *Testament of Man*. Fritz Dietrich records that at the Battle of the Somme a German ambulance was sent out under a devastating bombardment. "It was soon observed, and immediately the English airmen came lower and lower. This movement was a great act of chivalry; its effect was to silence the English artillery. Now ambulance after ambulance went out, protected by enemy planes, till all our wounded were brought back to safety."

Bruno Gutensohn, an airman, was chased by an English plane. "My gun jammed. All was over, I thought. I could see the Englishman watching my futile attempts to get the gun into action. The next moment he was gone, with a wave of the hand which told me as clearly as spoken words could do, 'I do not fight against unarmed men.' " No doubt there was chivalry on the other side, too.

A German attending an armistice service would not hear or see anything to hurt his feelings. The War will still be remembered, but without bitterness. I once sat next to Arthur Balfour at a public dinner in London, where a song about the blue bonnets coming over the border (Scots invading England) was sung. "Is there any other country where this could happen?" he said, much amused.

These "old unhappy far off things, and battles long ago" no longer trouble us at all. It is only in the Highlands that old feuds are never forgotten.

When the Head of the Campbells visited Glencoe, complaints were heard that it was "unco' soon after the massacre"—in the reign of William III.

December, 1938.

II

THE GENTLEMAN

When Mr. Wingfield Stratford sent me his new book, *The Making of a Gentleman*, I thought that after Smythe Palmer's comprehensive study, *The Ideal of a Gentleman*, there could hardly be room for another volume on the same subject. I was wrong. Mr. Wingfield Stratford has not only given us a good analysis of what the "grand old word" means or should mean, but he has drawn a series of portraits of the strange creatures who at one time or another have fancied themselves as perfect specimens of the type.

The gentleman is the ideal Englishman, the embodiment of our weekday religion. In the flesh he is often ridiculous and sometimes unedifying; but very few Englishmen would deny that they aimed at being gentlemen. If you told a bishop that he was no Christian, he would receive the rebuke with Christian humility; but if you said he was no gentleman, an explanation would be peremptorily called for.

It is agreed all over the world that the creation of this type is the chief contribution of our race to ethics. The word has been taken over by Continental nations, because there is no equivalent for it in any other language.

I read a book the other day in which one chapter was called "The Passing of the Gentleman." I do not agree. I think Wingfield Stratford is right when he says that the ideal was never more universally accepted in England than it is now. It has shed its adventitious connection with heraldry and property in land; it is no longer a class ideal, but it is more than ever a national ideal.

For that reason it is much to be regretted that a kind of inverted snobbishness has led many people to avoid the word. Such odious substitutes as *sahib* and white man should not be tolerated. The word "snob" has changed its meaning. It used to be a less offensive synonym of "cad," a word which is now generally avoided as conveying an unpardonable insult.

No analysis of the character of a gentleman is more often quoted than an elaborate paragraph by Cardinal Newman, which nevertheless is fundamentally wrong. For Newman supposes that the foundation of the gentleman's character is pride, and that he acts throughout for effect—to seem rather than to be. As a good Catholic, he prefers a dishonest Irish beggarwoman, "who is chaste and goes to Mass."

Our author thinks that the ideal of a gentleman is a product of Christianity. Certainly it is not easy to find examples outside our religion. Queen Victoria said that if she met King David in Heaven she would not recognize him; and surely, by our standards, the man after God's own heart was one of the champion cads of history. Think of his treatment of Uriah, Michal, Shimei, Joab and others.

In Greek history we fare no better. Achilles is a sulky savage, Ulysses a typical sailor, with a wife in every port and a lie for every emergency. A Roman triumph, culminating in the murder of the captive king or general, was the most brutally unchivalrous thanksgiving for victory ever devised.

The question has been raised whether in accepting and giving its blessing to such an alien ideal as chivalry the Church made one of its few mistakes. The combination of monk and knight is certainly an odd one. But though the chivalric ideal was not much like Tennyson's pictures of Arthur and his knights, the union of strength and gentleness in such a character as Malory's Sir Lancelot is both new and fine. Wordsworth's Happy Warrior is a modern description of the same type.

It would not be difficult to draw up a list of great gentlemen in history. King Alfred would win all votes. St. Louis of France, Sir Philip Sidney, Sir Walter Raleigh, General Havelock, Oates the Arctic explorer, would be included, and some of the young heroes who gave their lives in the Great War.

Among civilians, I think some of the finest gentlemen have been the best Anglican clergy. George Herbert is a beautiful example, but there have been very many others.

Among the men of letters of the last century, I think it will be generally agreed that Scott, Wordsworth and Shelley were gentlemen, and that Byron and Coleridge were not. For no one could contend that noble birth has much to do with it.

Pedigree stocks are valued and sought after because experience has shown that the easiest way to secure merit is to breed for it. When racing men and dog fanciers begin to disregard pedigrees, it will be time to discard eugenics and proclaim with the Irishman that one man is as good as another, "and better, too." But birth without works, like faith without works, is dead.

The superman, who in revolutionary times seizes power, is most unlikely to be a gentleman. For evil and good, his character is moulded on a savage inferiority complex, which has quenched in his mind every spark of gentleness, every wish to be just, fair or generous. "What do a million lives matter to me?" exclaimed Napoleon. The meanness and baseness of his character were displayed all through his career.

Perhaps his supreme act of caddishness was in leaving a legacy to a man who had tried to kill the Duke of Wellington. "A man must be a shabby fellow to do a thing like that," said the Duke, whose verdict on his great opponent was substantially the same as that of the Oxford don who was presented to Napoleon during the Peace of Amiens: "You could tell that he is not a university man!"

The typical English gentleman has often had

obvious defects. In the Middle Ages he was often a barbarian. Under Elizabeth was there not an element of play-acting in his courtiership and fighting and poetry? Sidney threw his life away: the flattery of Queen Elizabeth was humbug; and do we really believe in "the mythical sorrows of Shakespeare"?

Under French influence our social life became more civilized, though certainly not more moral; but Thackeray, who knew that period well, says that a fine gentleman of the time of Anne or George I would be quite unpresentable in a modern drawing-room. We are told of a nobleman who, when another peer made him too sweeping a bow, spat into his hat.

After Waterloo, when it was no longer the fashion to be French, there was a whole generation of extraordinary coarseness. Wellington, after seeing George IV and the Count d'Artois (Charles X) together, said that the "first gentleman of Europe" looked and behaved like the Frenchman's valet.

There is only one serious fault to find with the standardized product of our public schools. It is that which George Meredith and Matthew Arnold tried so hard to rub in. We cannot afford to go on saying to Britannia, "Be good, sweet maid, and let who will be clever."

December, 1938.

III

MORAL INDIGNATION

> That man should thus encroach on fellow man,
> Abridge him of his just and native rights,
> Moves indignation.

So wrote the gentle poet Cowper 150 years ago. He put it rather mildly. British blood has always boiled at the misdeeds of foreigners. Milton's organ voice booms out when he calls on the Almighty to avenge His slaughtered saints, the Waldensians. "We are glad," says Dryden, "to have God on our side to maul our enemies when we cannot do the work ourselves."

Gladstone's fervid and verbose eloquence was always on tap when atrocities were brought to his notice. First it was the Neapolitan prisons; then it was the *bashi-bazouks* in Bulgaria; then the unspeakable Turk was at his tricks again in Armenia. Friend or foe, it makes no difference. Wrong-doing must be dealt with faithfully.

Morel and Roger Casement found that the Belgians on the Congo were maltreating the natives. Cruelties of the same kind were brought home to the rubber-collectors in Brazil. Then came the unparalleled horrors of Bolshevism, which somehow or other roused less indignation than much

136

milder outbreaks of cruelty. But the attack on Abyssinia by the Italians roused us to fury. We had hoped that the ghastly experience of the Great War would have convinced all civilized nations that nothing of the kind must happen again, and the League of Nations was founded to give effect to this resolution. It was, therefore, with no common indignation that we witnessed an unprovoked assault upon one of the weakest members of the League.

Since then we have had to look on while Germany carried out two successful coups, both perhaps justifiable in themselves, but executed in a very high-handed fashion.

I am not ashamed of this British characteristic. If it is a foible, it is one which I share myself. I am as hot as anyone about some of these iniquities.

But we must beware of herd-contagion, especially when indignation is worked up for political reasons. The violent protest against the Hoare-Laval proposals with regard to Abyssinia obliged the Government to drop a scheme which might have secured for the unlucky Abyssinians better terms than they ultimately obtained. The Government knew that the resistance of the Abyssinians was about to collapse; the public did not know it. Whether Mussolini would have accepted the terms I do not know; the French and English diplomatists thought at the time that he might consent to them.

A foreign statesman once said that of all nations

the British are the most capable of going to war for an idea. I cannot recall a case when we have actually done so, though we have often been very near it. Our righteously indignant politicians are nearly always in opposition. Office cools the brain.

Do these indignant protests have any effect on foreign nations? That they may seriously embarrass our own Government we have seen; in the recent crisis they might well have been disastrous. Well-informed and temperately expressed criticisms may be really helpful, if they are allowed to reach those for whom they are intended. But under a dictatorship public opinion, if it can be said to exist, is inarticulate. The Press in those countries reports only violent and irresponsible utterances which inflame men's minds against us. The mischief done in this way can hardly be exaggerated.

No sensible person on the Continent doubts that we sincerely desire peace and good will. Bruce Lockhart found among all the smaller nations an earnest desire that Great Britain should be in a position to make her influence felt. They all look to us to prevent a war.

But many people on the Continent say: "You English are in the position of a gambler who, having raked in a very large stake, proposes that the party shall play for love for the rest of the evening. The nations are divided into the Haves and the Have-nots. You are the chief of the Haves."

We have held our Empire on two unwritten

conditions. First, that our army shall be kept too small to threaten any Continental nation, and, second, that we shall open our doors to alien commerce. When these conditions are violated, our position at once becomes dangerous.

We are also accused of having been none too just and merciful ourselves. Arnold Toynbee, in his great historical work, says that in our Colonies—in North America and Australia, for instance—we have almost exterminated the natives, while the Spanish colonies are still largely Indian. This, however, is not fair. Nomad hunters must disappear in the face of European settlement; half-civilized communities, like those of Mexico and Peru, can survive. The inhabitants of the Greater Antilles and of the Canaries were completely destroyed by the Spaniards.

But the slave trade is a terrible blot on our escutcheon. I will give two frightful instances, which show that not so long ago our humanity was only skin deep. My authority is George Bilainkin's *Front Page News, Once*:

"March 21, 1737.—They write from Antigua of the 15th January, that they continued executing the negroes concerned in the plot to subvert the Government: 69 had been executed, of whom five were broken on the wheel. Six were hung in chains upon gibbets and starved to death, of whom one lived nine nights and eight days without any sustenance, their heads then cut off and bodies burnt: 58 were chained to stakes and burnt, above 130 remain in prison."

"June 14, 1737.—St. Christopher's, ship Prince of Orange of Bristol, captain Japhat Bird. On the 14th of March we found a great deal of discontent among the men, which continued till the 16th. About five o'clock in the evening to our great amazement above a hundred of the men slaves jumped overboard, and it was with great difficulty that we saved as many as we did. We lost 33, as good men slaves as we had on board, who would not endeavour to save themselves, but resolved to die and sunk directly down. Many more were taken up almost drowned, some of them died since, but not to the owner's loss, they being sold before any discovery was made of the injury the salt water had done them."

The "ape and tiger" are not dead, even in our good-natured country, and a little more courtesy in criticizing our neighbours is desirable. We have the reputation of being censorious, and this both irritates other countries and makes them less willing to listen to us.

November, 1938.

IV

TORYISM AND THE FUTURE

THE original Tory Party may be said to have begun
in 1640 and ended in 1715. It was a Church
and King party; it differed from the Commonwealth party because it wished, in the words of
Hooker about the Anglican Reformation, "to
retain as much of former things as we may"—
which is always the aim of Conservatives.

"We live in a Church reformed, not in one made
new," as Laud said. But the average Tory was an
Anglican, not a Laudian; a royalist, not an abso-
lutist. The loyalist Bishop Morley, preaching at
the Restoration, said, "Despotical government is
that of the Turks and Muscovites, but political
government is and ought to be the government of
all Christian kings; I am sure it is of ours."

The party was wrecked for a time by the folly
of James II, which made it difficult for a church-
man to be a legitimist; Jacobitism died hard.
Queen Victoria, oddly enough, was a Jacobite.
"Do you think, Sir William Harcourt," she asked,
"that a people is ever justified in rebelling against
its sovereign?" "I am too loyal a subject of the
House of Hanover, ma'am, to say never," was Sir
William's answer.

Lord Hugh Cecil, in his little book on

Conservatism in the Home University Library, finds that Conservatism has three roots: (1) Distrust of untried change and love of what we are used to —natural Conservatism; (2) Church and King Toryism—respect for religion and lawful authority; (3) Patriotism.

This is a good summary of Conservatism as we have known it; but Church and King have not always been allies, and the Tories of Queen Anne's reign were anti-imperialists, as were the Tory opponents of the elder Pitt in George III's reign. Whig Little Englandism began with Fox.

Natural Conservatism will always shrink from the advice given in my hearing to Convocation at Oxford: "A leap in the dark? Any leap in the dark is better than standing still." It would be a dangerous experiment for a mountaineer overtaken by a fog.

Those only can be trusted to guide the future of a country to whom her past is dear. So at least the intelligent Tory believes. It was one of Burke's favourite themes that a nation is a society of which the dead, the living, and the yet unborn are all citizens, and that it is the custodian of all the accumulated wisdom of experience. Mazzini was not exactly a Conservative, but here he agreed with Burke:

"Those only should utter the sacred name of Progress whose souls possess intelligence enough to comprehend the past, and whose hearts possess sufficient poetic religion to reverence its greatness.

The temple of the true believer is not the chapel of a sect; it is a vast Pantheon."

Believing, as he does, that the history of a nation must be continuous, without any violent breaks with the past, the Conservative or Tory has no faith in revolution. We are now witnessing, as Thomas Mann wrote in 1930, "fanaticism regarded as a means of salvation, enthusiasm turned into epileptic energy, politics an opiate for the masses, a proletarian eschatology. Reason veils her face."

Toryism has never been the creed of the rich against the poor. The oligarchs of the eighteenth century were Whigs. The rich manufacturers of the industrial revolution were individualist Liberals. Disraeli tried to convince the country that his was the party of social rather than political reform, though he unscrupulously tried to "dish the Whigs" by a radical Reform Bill for which the country was not ready. His own head adorned the charger.

The typical Conservative to-day is the little man in a black coat; he lives in the suburbs.

Still, Conservatism has consistently stood for the right of private property and for the constitutional maxim, "No taxation without representation." As Lord Hugh Cecil says, it does not agree with the modern version of the parable of the Good Samaritan—that the Samaritan ran after the Priest and Levite, and took the horse of one and the purse of the other to give to the wounded man.

143

In reading his book I understood his political creed well enough. But when I took up the manifesto of several young Conservatives in Parliament entitled *Conservatism and the Future*, I felt that something new and strange has come over the party. These men do not seem to me to be Conservatives at all.

On the first page of this manifesto we are told that Conservatives "emphatically do not seek to conserve the present social system." A little later we read that "Tory principles sanction and indeed require an exercise of leadership and of compulsory authority more far-reaching than the principles of any other school of thought."

If the first of these utterances does not mean Socialism, and the second Fascism, what do they mean? The writers disclaim both imputations, but can they do so logically? They remind me of Herbert Spencer's *Man Versus the State*, in which as a sturdy individualist he calls Socialism the new Toryism, because in his opinion Toryism stands for order and regimentation and not for liberty.

The book contains no protests against reckless public expenditure, which is slowly strangling the prosperity of the country as it did in the Roman Empire. The end of this policy is inflation, which means national bankruptcy.

I am not a die-hard or a live-easy. My own tastes are severely simple ön principle, and on the whole I welcome the growing indifference to money and luxury which is very apparent in post-war England among my own class and the class above my own.

Still, I do not think it is the business of Conservatism to engage in a bribery competition with the Socialists. It is a losing game; Dick Turpin will always outbid Robin Hood, and the competition may make things worse for the victims, the unrepresented minority. Lord Hugh thinks that taxes which benefit one class exclusively should be paid by all, and this seems a sound principle.

Some of the essayists urge a policy of "Back to the Land." I wish this could be done, but the difficulties seem at present to be insuperable. It may be possible to encourage agriculture to a limited extent; but as long as the large majority of the population lives in towns, the town and not the country will call the tune. The only way to make England once more a nation of country-dwellers would be to destroy industrialism, and that process is not pleasant to think of.

What remains for Toryism to do? Natural Conservatism will be always with us, and it is strong in England. Now that, in consequence of the increased expectation of life and the dwindling birth-rate, we are becoming a nation of middle-aged and elderly people, we are less likely to be rushed into impetuous courses by the young, who are on the side of any party that will attack.

First, it may secure that social and political

changes shall be gradual, not violent, and in line with our national traditions. Revolutions cause great misery and end by provoking reactions, so that in the long run they effect very little.

Next, Toryism is determined not to lose the heritage of the past, though it may be preserved in forms which are less sacred than the treasure they contain. Among these traditions is certainly the Christian religion, which holds civilization together far more than is usually supposed.

As Bishop Berkeley, the philosopher, says: "Whatever the world thinks, he who hath not much meditated upon God, the human soul, and the supreme good may possibly make a thriving earthworm, but will most indubitably make a sorry patriot and a sorry statesman."

Thirdly, the Tory loves his country better than his class or his province. He hates class warfare and he disapproves of the present tendency for discontented provinces to break off from the central authority. Patriotism needs watching and purifying; so does every other loyalty; but it is not, as Ruskin rashly declared, "an absurd prejudice founded on an extended selfishness." Rather we may take to ourselves the words of Abraham Lincoln:

"With malice towards none; with charity for all; with firmness in the right, as God gives us to see the right, let us strive on to finish the work we are in."

December, 1938.

V

"THE ENGLISH ARE SOFT"

Now (1938) that the whole world, including invulnerable North America and pacific Scandinavia,
is busy squandering its resources in preparations for
the next war, it is probably useless to ask why and
against whom we are piling up armaments, instead
of putting our own house in order.

We cannot be surprised if certain foreign nations
suspect that we climbed down at Munich only
because we were not ready for a fray, and that we
mean to be ready next year.

I know some people are saying, "Are we afraid
to stand up to a bully? Are we acting honourably
in keeping the peace?" But apart from the fact that
we had no alliance with the Czechs, whose country
lies quite outside our sphere of influence, we ought
to have learned by this time that violence and
threats of violence can produce nothing but the
fruits of violence—more violence, more broken
treaties, more incalculable suffering for millions of
innocent people. "The wrath of man worketh not
the righteousness of God." It is not cowardice. It is
common sense and Christianity.

We all have a silly habit of personifying foreign
nations, as if they were individuals with disagreeable characters. But the Germans whom we should

kill if we went to war are worthy people much like ourselves, and they have no wish whatever to fight us.

They have a bad Government, but we cannot cure that by war. There will be a reaction. They will find out that butter is better than guns, and that some things are better than butter.

With this change may come a recovery of freedom. Liberty and militarism are incompatible.

This, however, is not my subject to-day. A letter signed by Lord Baldwin and others on September 10th pleaded for a more bracing moral tone in our people. The character of a nation is its greatest asset. Sir William Bragg broadcasted an address to the same effect.

Bismarck once said, "The English are a great people, but they are too soft." Well, the Germans did not find us very soft in the Great War, and they would not find us so now; but it must be confessed that duty and discipline are not words to conjure with in England as they are in Germany and Italy.

"Frenzied nationalism," we shall be told. I agree; but those who say (quoting Dr. Johnson unfairly) that patriotism is the last refuge of a scoundrel, are the kind of people whom I should be glad to see driven to their last refuge. Patriotism is not enough, as Edith Cavell said; but it was love of country that drew the rare tears from the eyes of Christ.

I agree with Lecky, that for many people "love of country is the only check for sectarian passions."

It is not the only check, but we cannot do without it.

If we do not believe that as a nation we are soft, lazy and self-indulgent, we should look at the figures of the amounts which our men spend every year on alcohol, tobacco and betting, and our women on frocks and cosmetics. Or consider the significance of the following, from Bruce Lockhart's new book:

"Göteborg is the home town of a huge concern which supplies ball bearings to every country in the world. The company has factories in most of the leading countries, and keeps very careful records of the respective efficiency of the workmen in the different nations. For the tiny ball bearings, the French women came first. In the other categories the Swedes just beat the Americans, with the Germans very little behind. 'And where do we come?' I asked. 'Easily last; I am afraid the British won't work, or have forgotten how to.' "

If this is true, it is not more guns or airplanes that will save us. As George Meredith says:

> Power! The hard man knit for action
> Reads each nation on the brow;
> Cripple, fool, and petrifaction
> Fall to him, are falling now.

We hear far too much about raising the standard of living. What we need is to raise the standard of good citizenship, and of pride in being in good training. "Thou, therefore, take thy share of hardship, as a good soldier of Jesus Christ."

There are two definitions of happiness in French writers which we may put side by side. "Happiness is measured by the number of rungs in the ladder of life which one discovers"—the ladder which leads up from earth to heaven (Sazaret). "Happiness consists in having many passions and the means to satisfy them" (Fourier).

But there seems to be another dangerous symptom. The other day I met a man who has given up a lucrative position in commerce because he could not stand the almost universal corruption and "graft" which he found in business. Things have become much worse, he thought, in the last ten years.

Another man told me that "the word of an Englishman" is no longer a proverb for truthfulness and rectitude among foreign nations. In fact, our business men have now a rather bad reputation.

In our relations at home, all trades-people, especially milliners, have a large proportion of bad debts, which of course they have to transfer, if they are to carry on, to their honest customers. The worst offenders seem to be rich women, or women who live as if they were rich by robbing their trades-people.

"It has long been a grave question," said Abraham Lincoln, "whether any Government not too strong for the liberties of its people can be strong enough to maintain its existence in great emergencies." It is for us to answer this question. It is for us to prove that a free nation can discipline itself as well as an authoritarian State under a dictator.

We have not proved it yet, and if we fail, liberty will be driven from her last refuge. Self-government will be discarded as an unsuccessful experiment, and all that our country has stood for in the eyes of the world for centuries will be cast aside as antiquated superstition.

November, 1938.

VI

ARE WE REALLY PATRIOTIC?

I SEE that Lord Esher has written to repudiate an article which he wrote a few months ago advocating a friendly deal with Germany. He withdraws it on the ground that it is impossible to deal with a man "whose word no man relies on."

I am beginning to fear that I may have to own myself wrong in my efforts to make my readers understand the German point of view. But I have a great dislike to bringing an indictment against a whole nation.

I do not even now understand why we were on the point of going to war last autumn. We had no pact with the Czechs, as France and Russia had; we could not have saved them by declaring war. The demand of the Sudeten Germans to join the Reich was quite reasonable.

I do not even think we ought to blame the Germans for wishing to piece together some of the fragments into which the Allies tore up the Austrian Empire, itself a German State, of course, in 1919. But the Germans may always be trusted to put themselves in the wrong, even when they have a case. Shameless perfidy is the worst of public crimes, since it makes confidence between nations impossible.

But in this article I wish to consider the peculiar

reactions of our people when international ethics are in question. Moral considerations have again and again deflected our policy to our disadvantage. Foreign nations seem unable to realize this fact, which is plainly written in our history.

Foreigners will never even begin to understand us until they realize that moral scruples often interfere with our politics, and that moral indignation often carries us off our feet. Our policy is difficult to predict for this reason, and we sometimes give violent offence to nations with whom it is to our interest to make friends. We are not tactful when we see red.

When our American colonists rebelled and called in the French to turn us out, public opinion at home was so divided that we fought the campaign in a half-hearted way and lost it.

In the wars against the French Revolutionary Government, our young intellectuals, including even Wordsworth, were strongly pro-French, until Napoleon showed his hand. Even then there were a few anti-patriots, as there always have been in this country. Herbert Spencer speaks of the anti-patriotic bias; it is a product almost peculiar to England. Our country's enemies, right or wrong, seems to be their motto. Boxer and Boer, Afridi and Afrikander, Mahdi and Matabele, all are "nations rightly struggling to be free." The Little Englander is an annoying person, but he is no hypocrite.

There was strong opposition to the Opium War with China, and to the Crimean War with Russia, but not strong enough to prevent two enterprises, the former iniquitous, the latter unnecessary, and therefore wicked. I am not suggesting for a moment that we have always been right, but that when we have done wrong we have done it with a bad conscience.

Gladstone made a present of the Ionian Islands to the weak kingdom of Greece, a generous act which has few parallels. The Greeks have never forgotten it.

We drove Turkey into the arms of Germany by our vehement indignation at Abdul Hamid's methods of government. We alienated Italy, a nation which had always been our friend, by our anger at the wanton attack upon Abyssinia. It is ridiculous to say that our indignation was hypocritical, a cloak for dark designs. We in England know well that it was not so. Our neighbours will not believe in our disinterestedness, partly because such motives do not count in their own political actions, and partly because our comparatively decent behaviour has hitherto stood us in good stead.

Our neighbours may pretend to dislike us, but they do not really want to see our Empire destroyed. There have been no coalitions against us. The Greeks had a proverb. "When the oak falls, every man gathers wood." The fall of the British oak would plunge the world into chaos and bloodshed.

Our combination of conquest and generous government has had some odd results. What is the only flourishing French colony, the only part of the world where the French population increases? Canada. We have helped the Dutch to multiply in South Africa, and have added several millions to the swarming population of Egypt. In India the native population has doubled under our rule.

The Americans, following the same methods, have made Cuba and Puerto Rico for the first time Spanish islands, and are preparing to quit the Philippines, for which they have done much. This is not the old imperialism, but we are quite content to have it so.

Are we really a very patriotic people? If one side of patriotism is malignant hatred of other nations, we are much less patriotic than the Irish, the Poles and the Balkan States. In fact, we are the worst haters in the world; our memories are very short. But the Prime Minister was right when he said the other day that we should fight to the death for our liberties. We should not care to live if we were terrorized by secret police. Perhaps we shall not realize how much we love our country till it is menaced with destruction.

Our sense of humour forbids some flamboyant demonstrations of patriotism. An American, on strike against Prohibition, knocked down a fellow citizen, who, being in the same condition, had fallen in the gutter and had wiped his hands on an American flag hanging out of a shop window. Arrested by the police, the assaulter bethought himself of pleading that the insult to "Old Glory" was too much for him. The magistrate left his seat to shake his hand, and a subscription was raised to buy him a house.

That would not happen in England. Flag-waving seems to us in rather bad taste. We love our country as a man loves his wife. He does not go about praising her beauty and her virtues, and he is quite willing that other men should think their wives the best women in the world, though of course they are mistaken.

We are not very punctilious about the point of honour. It is significant that we were the first nation to give up duelling. The action of the Duke of Wellington, who "plumped down" on his knees to an allied Spanish general, who would not take orders from an Englishman, is characteristic. A Frenchman or German would have refused, and lost the battle.

Of course it is mere common sense that, having everything to lose and nothing to gain by war, we must keep the peace at almost any price. We ought not to forget that there have been times when we were arrogant and boastful enough. Milton's complacent remark that when there is anything great to be done God reveals it first to his Englishmen, makes us blush now. Some of *Punch's* cartoons when Palmerston was Prime Minister make us squirm. All this arrogance is quite over, but it is remembered against us, however mild our present manners may be.

March, 1939.

HISTORY

I

OUR ALIEN CIVILIZATION

THERE is one very queer thing about the civilization of modern Europe. It has the appearance of being borrowed. In our divine worship we sing hymns, not about our own country, its glories and its trials, but about the ancient Hebrews. We have no hymns about the Spanish Armada or the Battle of Waterloo: we rejoice over the discomfiture of Sehon, King of the Amorites, and Og, the King of Basan; we read the splendid description of the deliverance of Hezekiah from Sennacherib.

If a stranger were to visit our public schools, he would be equally surprised to find the boys studying, not Shakespeare, Milton and Burke, but Homer, Sophocles and Demosthenes.

Why should these two little peoples, who lived 2,000 or 3,000 years ago, still form the staple of our higher education and of our religion? Does it not look as if we had never really found ourselves? Can we seriously maintain that Dante, Shakespeare and Goethe are less worthy of study than the Athenians of the fifth and fourth centuries before Christ, or that Joshua was a greater general than Marlborough?

There is of course a historical explanation.

When Europe awoke from the long night of the Dark Ages, with the classics in her hand, a return to antiquity was the only road of recovery. "Back to Greece and Rome" was the cry of the Latin races, which had once belonged to the Roman Empire. "Back to Palestine" was the reply of the north, which did not wish to be paganized. But the north did not reject Greece.

As Matthew Arnold said, we have been under two influences ever since; we have Hebraized and Hellenized. The two ideals are very different, and our national character is a queer amalgam. Modern Europe has added three ingredients of its own, which are neither Hebrew nor Greek—chivalry, romance and industrialism.

Such is our civilization; it is not indigenous in the sense in which Hellenism and Hebraism were indigenous.

The Greeks were of mixed origin, a fusion of northern invaders with the southern race whom they found in occupation. For some reason which has never been explained, they were both physically and intellectually superior to any other race that we know of.

Their physical beauty lives for us in their statues, which are, no doubt, idealized; but no such models could be found in any modern civilized nation. As for education, every Athenian could read and write, and the populace which enjoyed the Greek drama was on a rather different level from those who go to see American films. But of course the whole of Greece was not like Athens, and after Greece lost her freedom, the Romans thought that the Greeks were too clever by half even for their own interest, and not to be trusted in any relation of life.

What have we still to learn from this remarkable people, whose supremacy in literature has been acknowledged by the best judges? "In every branch of letters and learning," says Cicero, "they are our masters." "Beside Æschylus and Sophocles I am nothing," said Wordsworth. "The period between the birth of Pericles and the death of Aristotle," Shelley wrote, "is undoubtedly the most memorable in the history of the world." "The Greeks were the beginners of nearly everything, Christianity excepted, of which the modern world makes its boast." This is from John Stuart Mill.

How did they do it? Largely because speech was free. The Greeks were great talkers, not great readers, and they discussed everything under the sun. There was no system of espionage, no Gestapo and concentration camps, no Holy Inquisition, though Plato, I regret to say, would have liked to establish one.

Under a tyranny there may be a small cultivated class, as in France under Louis XIV, but not a civilized nation. How little Germany has contributed to learning and literature since the Great War! In Greece, for some 800 years, ending with the closing of the schools of Athens by Justinian, the human spirit had been free to inquire into all things in heaven and earth.

The extreme simplicity of their habits would have astonished us. When Plato went to Sicily he records with displeasure that the people there have two square meals a day. That this abstemiousness is good for health cannot be doubted. I have often noticed the longevity of the ancient Greeks, compared with modern times down to our own generation, when the duration of life has notably increased.

One of their favourite maxims was "Nothing too much." We have a thoroughly vulgar craze for records, a taste which is still stronger in America. Professionalism is spoiling one game after another. Tables of averages are not at all good for cricket.

They wished their surroundings to be beautiful. We have evolved an ugly civilization, which accordingly does not attract much affection. A popular adage of the Greeks makes beauty the second in rank of human goods, the first being health. We should think this is a very odd estimate.

They were not perfect—far from it. They committed suicide as a race by the continual storms in a teacup between two tiny States, by the frequent massacres which attended their civil discords, and by their ruinous practice of female infanticide.

They were hard, as the Italians of the Renaissance were hard, and sometimes very cruel. It is a curious fact that the flowering times of the arts have seldom been humane. The parallel with Mediæval Italy has often been drawn.

The belief in progress, though often a mere superstition, has encouraged us Western Europeans to advocate many causes—and attempt many reforms. The Greeks had no belief in progress. They looked for their golden age, if they thought of one, in the past rather than in the future. History, they thought, is a series of vast cycles, and they had happened on a descending curve. When we think how many of the noblest lives among us are devoted to some cause or other, we cannot help seeing in the absence of such enthusiasms a sign of inferiority.

Shall we go on reverencing the Greeks and the Hebrews as we have done for centuries? Probably not to the same extent. We have learned from them most of what they have to teach us, and we ought now to be able to stand on our own feet. But in different ways these two cultures represent permanent enrichments of our human heritage which must never be forgotten.

These achievements are very rare in history, and unfortunately they do not last long. It is lamentable to think that by far the greater part of Greek literature and art has perished without leaving a trace. There have been times when to burn an ode of Sappho or smash a statue of Pheidias was considered a laudable action.

July, 1939.

II

MEDITERRANEAN MEDITATION

GEOGRAPHERS tell us that the Mediterranean type
of climate is confined to a few favoured spots
scattered over various parts of the world. Besides
the coasts of the inland sea of Europe, it is found in
California, in the district round Capetown, in
southern Chile, and in the south-west of Australia.
To me it seems that those who live in this climate
are greatly to be envied.

Robert Browning said, "O to be in England now
that April's here," and I will not differ from him.
The late spring and early summer in England should
satisfy anybody. But for about four months in the
year the climate of Great Britain, though healthy
enough, is depressing and disagreeable. My spirits
go up as soon as I catch sight of the Mediterranean.
It is not so much the warmth, for Greece can be
very cold in spring, and I shall never forget a day
at Alassio when the wind was blowing down from
the Alps. It is the sun, the clear air, the grand
mountain scenery, and above all the incomparable
friendly sea, with its rich colours.

One thing one notices at once in this tideless sea.
On our coasts all our harbours are at the mouths
of rivers, so that fishermen may go out with the

current and come in with the tide. In the Mediterranean river mouths are avoided.

The Greek islands are simply the highest points of a submerged mountain-chain, of which Crete is the most elevated part. The valleys, formed by soil washed down from the mountains, are very small. How do the people live? Even the mainland consists chiefly of rocks.

I have sometimes wondered what Pericles or Demosthenes would have thought if they could have stood on the Acropolis of Athens, as I did recently, and looked at the city beneath them. It is four times as populous as the Athens which they knew. There is no gap between Athens and the Piræus, and the houses now cluster round the foot of Lycabettus, which rises out of the streets like the famous rock at Rio.

Those who disparage freedom should remember that this great capital, which now ranks with Marseilles, Barcelona and Naples as one of the largest four cities on the Mediterranean, was 150 years ago a poor village. How the people live is a mystery, but there they are. A large suburb is inhabited by the refugees from Asia Minor, who were expelled by the Turks after the Great War. No European Power tried to stop this outrage, which destroyed all the churches to which St. John wrote in the Apocalypse, and obliterated cities which had been Greek for nearly 3,000 years.

The Western Powers showed more sympathy

with Greece 100 years earlier. The Turks, unable to crush the insurgent Greeks, who had the command of the sea, called in the help of Mohammed Ali, the independent viceroy of Egypt. There was every prospect that the Greeks would be exterminated, and the Peloponnese colonized by Egyptians and negroes. This was too much for a nation of which the ruling class had received a classical education. Admiral Codrington, without the formality of a declaration of war, wiped out the Turkish-Egyptian fleet in the harbour of Navarino in 1827, and the French landed troops who completed the deliverance of Greece.

In 1927 the Greek colony in London celebrated the centenary of Navarino by a banquet in London. I was one of the invited speakers. The other speakers had been requested by the Foreign Office to say nothing to hurt the feelings of Brother Turk—but I had not been warned. I let myself go, and ended by saying that I hoped to see the Œcumenical Patriarch celebrating Christian worship at St. Sophia.

The Greeks were hugely delighted. My speech was telegraphed to Athens and fully reported in the Greek newspapers. Soon after I received an illuminated address from the refugee committees, declaring in flowery modern Greek that the glorious name of "Inky" ought to be inscribed in letters of gold with those of Byron, Codrington and Gladstone. Finally they gave me a medal.

The modern Greeks have acquired the goodwill of the old firm. They are as much Greeks as the countrymen of Mussolini are Romans. They have made the most praiseworthy attempts to revive the old language, though I do not think they speak it. Notices intended to be understood by all are in impeccable ancient Greek, such as "Keep to the right," and, at a level crossing, "Caution ! Danger ! ! Death ! ! !" For me, it is a comfort to find foreigners who put up their notices in an intelligible language !

I have just come back from the beautiful island of Melos, a Dorian colony which was wantonly attacked and annexed by Athens in 416 B.C. Thucydides describes the preliminaries in detail—a powerful expedition, insolent demands on the helpless islanders, and the sequel.

The speeches of the Athenian envoys might have been spoken to-day by Hitler or Mussolini. "You know as well as we do that right, as the world goes, is only a question between equals. The strong do what they can; the weak suffer what they must."

The Melians: "The privilege of being allowed to appeal to justice is the protection of all. You may come to need it yourselves."

The Athenians: "We are not afraid of that."

The Melians: "Do you wish to make enemies of all neutrals, who will conclude that some day you will attack them?"

The Athenians: "We do not think that other

169

nations will take precautions against us. For you the alternative is submission or destruction."

The Melians: "We know our danger; but heaven defends the right, and the Spartans will help us."

The Athenians: "To appeal to heaven is nonsense, and the Spartans will not help you."

The Melians: "We have been a free country for seven hundred years, and we will not surrender our independence. We wish to remain neutral in the war between Athens and Sparta."

No help came. The Athenians put to death all the men, and sold the women and children into slavery.

Thucydides wastes no words over this shocking atrocity, but he adds grimly: "The same winter the Athenians resolved to send an expedition against Sicily." Not a man or a ship returned from that expedition. This last act of aggression sealed the doom of the Athenian Reich. A few years later Athens surrendered to the Spartan general Lysander, and was treated more mercifully than she had any right to expect.

April, 1939.

III

THE PAPACY

THE Papacy is the one political institution which will probably survive even the British monarchy, which might conceivably be upset by a very self-willed or imprudent King. "Never" is a word which a wise man will never use; otherwise we might predict that a time will never come when there will be no Pope.

The Roman Church, which is the heir of the Roman Empire, has obeyed the same law, if it is a law, which transformed the Republic into the autocracy of Diocletian and the Byzantine emperors. But one right is still withheld: the Pope cannot nominate his successor. Thus the evils of a hereditary dynasty are avoided.

The choice of the Supreme Pontiff by the College of Cardinals is now as good a guarantee against a bad ruler as could be devised. But it has not always been so.

I have been reading *The Triple Crown*, by Valérie Pirie. It is an account of the Papal Conclaves from the fifteenth century to the present day. The greater part of the book is an amazing story of shameless intrigue, corruption, perfidy and crime.

Some of the Mediæval Popes were blackguards of the deepest dye, sunk in debauchery, gluttony, avarice, and every other vice. The word "nepotism" preserves the memory of the practice of almost all the Popes, to enrich the young men who were politely called their nephews. It was a recognized thing that a new Pope should at once make his nephew a Cardinal. Paul III bestowed the hat on several of his grandsons, the eldest of whom was fifteen.

The avarice of the Popes in the Middle Ages was insatiable. All ecclesiastical dignities were openly sold; taxes on disorderly houses brought in a steady revenue; and there was a tariff for the absolution of all crimes, to which Sixtus IV added a plenary indulgence to anyone who killed a Venetian. In the reign of Leo X, the magnificent Medici Pontiff painted by Raphael, indulgences were staked for in gambling hells.

It has been argued that only a divine institution could have survived such scandals. But Dante was nearer the mark when he said that Constantine did the Church infinite harm, not by being converted, but by making the Popes rich. Before the end of the fourth century the streets of Rome ran with blood at the election of Pope Damasus, nicknamed "the ear-picker of ladies," and the Prefect of Rome said that he would himself turn Christian if they would make him Pope.

The romantic proceedings at the Conclave are well known—all doors locked and sealed, all outlets boarded up. Gregory X made a rule that if the Cardinals could not agree within three weeks they were to be reduced to bread and water, but this was soon repealed. Scrutinies of the votes are taken twice a day, and the crowd outside watches for the smoke which rises from a certain chimney when the voting papers are burnt. Finally, one of the Sacred College appears on a balcony, and announces in Latin, "I give you good tidings of great joy. We have a Pope." The name follows.

The sovereigns of the chief Catholic countries had a right to veto one candidate. This right was last exercised by Francis Joseph of Austria, who forbade the election of Cardinal Rampolla. Pius IX was elected in a hurry to forestall the Austrian veto, which duly arrived just too late.

In 1458 Pius II needed one vote to make up his two-thirds majority. Cardinal Colonna, a supporter of the Archbishop of Rouen, who had just, as scrutineer, falsified the numbers, was preparing to change over when the Archbishop of Rouen and one of his friends flung themselves upon him and tried in vain to prevent him by main force from voting. The next moment, since Piccolomini was now Pope, they all fell on their faces before him in homage.

In 1513 many of the Cardinals, wishing to temporize until they knew which way the wind was blowing, began by voting for the most impossible outsider in the College. Unfortunately, thirteen of them selected the same nonentity, who was very nearly elected.

Some of the Cardinals had never been ordained. The astute minister of Pius IX, Cardinal Antonelli, was in this position, which, considering his private life, was perhaps just as well.

Did the people of Rome resent being under such unworthy rulers? Sometimes they did, but they did not always hate the worst of them. In 1522, by a strange oversight, the College chose a Puritan ascetic, Adrian VI, who was quite wrongly suspected of being a miser. When he died the Romans put up a statue to his physician, and inscribed on it the words, "To the saviour of his country." But the cruel persecutor, Paul IV, was detested as he deserved, and the corpse of the horrible Borgia Pope was dishonoured. The warlike Julius II seems to have been rather popular.

My taste for vital statistics has led me to a curious inquiry. Between 1455 and 1600 there were twenty-four Popes, who reigned on an average six years each. It is true that some of them were elderly men, and that the habits of many of them were not conducive to longevity. One of them, Alexander VI, was poisoned, or rather poisoned himself accidentally. But did the others all die natural deaths? I think anyone familiar with the subject would say that it is impossible. Several Popes were almost certainly poisoned.

This may seem incredible, when we remember the sanctity attached to the Pope's person; but it is far from being so in reality. Poisoning in Renaissance

Italy was a fine art. About 1600 a man confessed voluntarily that he had poisoned two Popes. The priest withheld absolution till he had consulted the Pope, Clement VIII. The Pope allowed him to be absolved, but thought it prudent to remove him from further temptation, so he was handed over to the Inquisition.

Times are changed when we come to the gentle Pius VII, whom Napoleon bullied and insulted, and to the long and inglorious reign of Pius IX, whom the countryfolk in Italy believed to have the "evil eye." He was an ignorant man of blind, uncritical faith; no hoax was too gross for his acceptance. In his later years he posed as "the prisoner of the Vatican," and received welcome tributes of money, especially from South America. In reality he was not a prisoner at all.

His successor, Cardinal Pecci, who took the name of Leo XIII, restored to the Holy See the respect which it had lost. He was a scholar, a statesman and a man of high character. From his pontificate dates the increased influence of the Roman Catholic Church, which is especially noticeable in the Protestant countries, England, Holland, Germany and the United States.

The compromise which has at last been reached between the Vatican and the Italian Government leaves the precincts of the Vatican as a tiny independent State. The Holy Father owes allegiance to no man; his authority over his world-wide subjects is not complicated by any embroilment with secular politics.

Never before, since the conversion of Constantine, has his position, as a spiritual ruler, been so favourable as it is now. Even if Italy were engaged in an unjust war with another Catholic Power, he could maintain a dignified though embarrassed neutrality.

The Eternal City will never again be a world capital, and the dream of a universal Church is as unsubstantial as that of a universal empire. But this unique institution still has a great future before it.

It knows that human nature does not change; and whenever hopes are disappointed, whenever popular catchwords such as "democracy," "social-ism," "humanism" and "progress" lose their attractiveness and begin to sound hollow, many will take refuge under the shelter of a tradition which touches human nature at so many points.

"The Church," said Theodore Beza to a monarch of his day, "is an anvil which has worn out many hammers."

February, 1939.

IV

VOLTAIRE

THE threat of the Roman Catholic authorities to take disciplinary measures against a well-known English author for his book on Voltaire has revived public interest in a monstrous miscarriage of justice which aroused Voltaire's indignation to such an extent that, after three years of hard work, posthumous justice was done to the unfortunate victim. It was like the Dreyfus case, only worse.

In 1762 Jean Calas, an aged Calvinist and a resident of Toulouse, was accused of murdering his son in order to prevent him from becoming a Catholic. The son, Marc-Antoine, had wished to enter a learned profession; but no Protestant was allowed to practise either law or medicine, and a Huguenot pastor had been hanged in that very year at Toulouse. After losing money at play, the young man hanged himself in his father's shop. His brother found him and cut him down, but he was dead.

Unfortunately, the family at first concealed the truth from the authorities. Suicides, by the law of France, were drawn naked through the streets and then hung in chains. So they reported that they had found him lying dead.

Toulouse had long been a centre of fanaticism.

Rabelais makes his hero leave the University of Toulouse because it was "in the habit of roasting its professors like herrings, his own blood being hot enough to need no further heating." In 1562, 4,000 Protestants were massacred there. This exploit was celebrated every year by the Catholics, but this was a centenary, and the Pope extended the privileges of the festival for eight days.

On the news of the young man's death it was decided to bury him with great pomp as a martyr, processions were organized, and the whole family of Calas were arrested as principals or accessaries to the murder.

At the trial of Jean Calas, one of the magistrates was censured for "partiality to the accused," and the defending counsel was suspended. Even so, five out of thirteen judges voted for acquittal, because there was not a scrap of evidence against the father, a feeble old man who could hardly have strangled his able-bodied son, even if he had wished to do so.

Nothing was left undone to force Jean Calas to confess. He was stretched on the rack, subjected to the water-torture, and then broken on the wheel, his arms, legs and ribs smashed with an iron bar. Finally, he was strangled and his body burned. Because he protested his innocence to the end his widow was acquitted. The son, Pierre, was shut up in a monastery, from which he escaped. The two daughters were confined in convents. The youngest son fled to Geneva.

Voltaire, always prudent and cautious, did not act till he had seen and questioned the sons, Pierre and Donat. Then he was convinced that a shocking judicial murder had been committed. The old father, as it happened, was not at all a bigoted Protestant, and Marc-Antoine, so far from wishing to change his religion, had severely blamed Louis, another brother, for doing so.

The agitation for the repeal of the sentence, conducted mainly by Voltaire, was much like Zola's persistent efforts to rehabilitate Captain Dreyfus. The case advanced slowly. First, the sentence was quashed on a matter of form. Then, before the royal Court of Appeal, just three years after the execution of Calas, the case was retried, and the defence was heard. The accused, both dead and living, were acquitted, and the Parlement of Toulouse was ordered to erase the record from its books.

The consequences of this famous victory were not great till the Revolution, but the ill-treatment of Protestants was certainly mitigated.

How came these things to be done in what was then, as some think it is now, the most civilized country in the world? To begin with, criminal justice was still cruel in the eighteenth century. Pressing to death, the *peine forte et dure*, was still employed in England to force prisoners to plead. Readers of *Old Mortality* remember how the torture of the boot was used in Scotland under the Stuarts: Guy Fawkes fared no better than Calas.

Since the Great War, torture of one kind or another has come back to Europe. Even in America we have heard of inquisitions in prison by "the third degree."

But we must not shirk the main question. How is it that the religion of love has been, in a sense, responsible for some of the worst cruelties and injustices that have ever disgraced humanity? No one, certainly not Voltaire, would think of laying the blame on the divine Founder of our religion. Christ saw the beginning of the evil when two of his disciples wished to call down fire from heaven upon a Samaritan village. "Ye know not what spirit ye are of," He said to them.

But the Church has persecuted more cruelly than any other religion. Paganism was tolerant, except when the suspicions of a tyrant were aroused. Some of the persecutions of Christians were more like Russian pogroms than the organized and sustained activities of the Inquisition.

Fanaticism is the cruellest spirit in the world. It will not listen to reason or argument. "Do not I hate them, O Lord, that hate thee? Yea, I hate them with a perfect hatred." So says one of the Psalms, which we sing in church without thinking much of the meaning.

We do not want to kill people who differ from us on other subjects. But our religious beliefs are propped upon a traditional scaffolding, and many of us are intensely annoyed if the stability of this scaffolding is called in question. The average Catholic relies on the infallibility of his Church, which he has usually accepted without investigation. To own that his Church has been in the wrong, and has sanctioned heinous crimes, is almost impossible for him. If such suspicions enter his mind, he repulses them like the suggestions of sensuality. The hierarchy, therefore, can usually rely on the support of the laity even when its policy is morally most questionable.

There was a proverb in the middle ages, "If you have offended a priest, kill him—for he is a terrible enemy." It was Judas, the layman, who repented and went and hanged himself; Caiaphas, we may be sure, never thought of doing such a thing. What can we say except that the noblest ambitions may betray a man to the lowest fall? There have been terrible characters who seem to have conquered the world and the flesh only to sell themselves to the devil.

It is not an easy question to answer whether the State ever has the right to suppress poisonous opinions by force. There are a few things which a man is not allowed to advocate even in England— assassination, for instance, and unnatural vice. But who is to decide whether the opinions really are poisonous? Respectable public opinion. When this is divided, there must be toleration.

Persecution is not always ineffective. Protestant-ism was destroyed in Spain and Italy, checked in France and Bohemia. But the misdeeds of the persecutor, whether in Church or State, come home to roost sooner or later. You cannot kill ideas, says Loisy, with blows of a stick. A man may be forced to unsay, but not to unsee.

I have always liked Voltaire as much as I loathe Rousseau. There never was a man who loved liberty and hated cruelty more than this queer little mummy of a man who was always oscillating between life and death, and who lived to be eighty-four, enjoying life to the last.

But he has always been a *bête noire* to churchmen. After the Restoration in 1814, some partisans of the orthodox Bourbons even desecrated his grave in the Pantheon and threw his remains into a ditch.

He was not an atheist; he quite honestly believed in God. "I wish to love God," he said. "I seek in Him my Father; but they show me a tyrant whom I ought to hate."

Still, it was perhaps a little rash for a Catholic to say that "the Voltairean movement may yet have an immense part to play in leading the world on to a new age of reason and religion." For this man, who had a great admiration for the Quakers whom he met in England, hated the Jesuits; and such sentences as the following were not unlikely to give offence:

"When the English learn that in France young fellows, notorious for debauchery, are raised to bishoprics by women's intrigues; that they make love in public; that they spread daily luxurious

182

dinners, and go from them to pray for the guidance of the Holy Ghost, the English thank God that they are Protestants. But of course the English are heretics, fit only to be burned; so the devil take them."

The last sentence is obviously ironical.

"There are some things too serious to be talked of seriously." Voltaire, "not having a hundred thousand moustaches at his command," was obliged to use the rapier, not the bludgeon, and there was no parrying his sudden thrusts. We all know that the English shot Admiral Byng because "they think it expedient now and then to execute an admiral *pour encourager les autres*"; and Tacitus himself would have been proud of his summing up of Mazarin. "He was guilty of all the good that he did not do." Mr. Noyes shows that he made great efforts to save Admiral Byng's life.

But ecclesiastics do not like those who "make fun of holy things." For instance, we are told that a saint was visited by two angels, whom he politely asked to sit down. "*Nous n'avons pas de quoi*," they replied. So Charles Lamb piously hoped that his flogging schoolmaster, Dr. Boyer, might be "wafted to bliss by little cherub boys, all head and wings, with no bottoms to reproach his sublunary infirmities."

Churchmen prefer Milton's account of the cold collation ("no fear lest dinner cool") at which Adam entertained the Archangel Raphael. Both were seated, somehow, and were waited on by Eve, who stood behind them without a stitch of clothing on.

Thomas Hardy, after hearing a sermon by a modernist divine, said that he should go home and "read that moderate man, Voltaire." Moderate is not the epithet that I should have chosen for this hard hitter; but assuredly there were vital parts of the Christian religion which he would never have consented to give up.

I do not think that he was in any real sense of the word a religious man. There is nothing in his writings to suggest that he even understood the longing for communion with God in which religion consists. Natural religion, so much in the mouths of eighteenth-century rationalists, is often neither natural nor religious. Still less could this born rebel, this despiser of authority, have even been a loyal Catholic. His dislike of the arguments on which Pascal based his submission to the authority of the Church is very significant. But like most men who have been brought up in the Church of Rome, he shrank from the idea of dying under the ban of the Church, and, like Shakespeare, he had a horror of the idea that his dead body might be dishonoured— as at last it was.

He thought that the part of the Jews in history had been much exaggerated. But in truth the whole of the Old Testament is a refusal to give any answer except "Yes" to the question which is asked in the book of Genesis: "Shall not the judge of all the

earth do right?" And this was the best side of
Voltaire.

He would make no compromise with injustice and
cruelty, even when supported by all the power of
organized religion. We sometimes forget how
monstrous were the abuses which sheltered themselves under the authority of the Church under the
old régime. The fact that the King's mistress,
Madame Pompadour, offered to procure for Voltaire a Cardinal's hat is a measure of the corruption
which excited the indignation of the Revolution
against the Church.

He was no revolutionary, and would certainly
not have joined the "Mountain" if he had lived to
see the Revolution; but he showed up the scandals
which were bringing disgrace upon the name of
Christianity, and reminded his contemporaries that
the "weightier matters of the law are justice, mercy
and truth."

November, 1938.

V

BURIED CITIES

IF a flourishing seaside town in England—say, Scarborough or Eastbourne—were suddenly swallowed up, and excavated 1,000 years hence, what would our descendants think of the manners and customs of the English in 1939?

The world is now changing so rapidly that it is impossible to guess.

There is one buried city which has suffered the fate of Pompeii within living memory. St. Pierre, the capital of the French colony of Martinique, was obliterated with all its 30,000 inhabitants by an eruption of Mont Pélée. The site has, I believe, been almost undisturbed so far, partly because a deadly snake, the *fer de lance*, has taken possession. As St. Pierre is said to have been morally rather more depraved than Port Said, the antiquarians of the future may find as much to shock them as is now concealed from curious eyes in a locked room of the Museum at Naples and in the Vico del Lupanare at Pompeii.

It is a thrilling experience to stand, as I have just been doing, in the streets of a town where time suddenly stood still in August, A.D. 79. Vesuvius, of whom nobody had been much afraid, gave some notice of his intentions, and most of the inhabitants seem to have escaped from the town, though whether they got away beyond the radius of the storm of stones and ashes is very doubtful.

Many hundreds must have perished in Pompeii. The bodies lie singly or in groups, eighteen in one cellar. Liquid plaster has been poured into the cavity in the mud left by the decomposed corpses, and every feature is preserved of the unfortunates who died gasping for breath. Among the victims is a chained dog.

What should we think of Pompeii as a town, compared with modern seaside resorts? The comparison is hardly fair, for the place was only buried in ashes and mud, and in the third century it was used as a quarry from which statues, marbles and columns were drawn out and set up at Rome.

But the public buildings were finer than we should expect to find in an English town of the same size. The forum is a rectangular piazza, 466 by 125 feet. It was surrounded by a cloister; at one end was an imposing temple of Jupiter; opposite to this were three large halls used as municipal buildings, and on the west a basilica, 130 by 65 feet, used as a stock exchange and for miscellaneous purposes.

There were three public baths (there may have been more, for quite one-third of the town is still covered). These were popular clubs, with exercise grounds and other attractions, and adorned with fine works of art. There were cold baths, tepid baths, and hot Turkish baths, scientifically heated by hot-air flues.

There were two theatres, the larger of which could hold 5,000 people, one quarter of the whole population. Over 10,000 could enjoy the inhuman spectacles in the amphitheatre, where friezes give realistic pictures of the arms carried by different classes of gladiators, and of the manner in which a conquered swordsman appealed for mercy to the spectators. One kneels to have his throat cut; the umpire intervenes to give another time to make his appeal.

Nearly all the rooms of private houses are decorated with frescoes painted on the walls, many of them of great beauty. There is a famous mosaic pavement representing Alexander the Great and King Darius at the Battle of Issus. In a country house outside the walls, lately unearthed, there is a splendid series of pictures representing initiation into the mysteries—a most interesting find.

There were many rich men in Pompeii, whose houses are large and sumptuous. There was nothing to see from the outside—a plain doorway leading through a short passage to a large hall with a tank in the middle, into which the rain was conveyed through a square opening in the roof. At one side of the hall was a row of bedrooms, beyond it the family living-room and a richly decorated dining-room.

Beyond this again was an open court and cloister,

enclosing a flower garden and adorned with statues. At the far end was a small door into the street, by which the owner might escape from unwelcome visitors. There were no windows on the ground floor looking out on the street, and the occupants may not have got quite enough fresh air; but in Italy the sun is an enemy, and the large houses on the whole must have been very comfortable.

The streets are narrow, like those of our old towns. They are well paved, and have sidewalks for foot passengers. The most curious feature is the large stepping-stones in all the chief thoroughfares. The tracks of carriage wheels pass between them; the horses must have stumbled across them somehow.

The Romans were in the habit of scratching or painting on their house-walls a great many things for which we use paper. The keeper of a gaming hell writes his accounts on the wall. Lovers record their unedifying adventures. Advertisements of forthcoming entertainments are made public. An overseer writes up the weight of wool to be spun by female slaves, and gives the names of the girls: Vitalis, Florentina, Amaryllis, Januaria, Heracla, Maria, Lalagia, Damalis and Doris.

One man tells us that he has a cold; another that anyone who does not ask him to supper is a brute and a barbarian. A third wonders that walls on which so much nonsense is written have not fallen down.

It seems that municipal elections were being held.

This brings us very near to Pompeii. Recommendations of candidates were not scratched on the walls, but painted in bold red letters by men employed for the purpose. Sometimes a prominent citizen "asks you to vote for so-and-so; he is a good man." Sometimes the various trade guilds nominate a candidate. The Unions of Dyers and Cleaners, of Bakers, of Goldsmiths, of Fruiterers, of Greengrocers, of Muleteers, of Cooks, have all chosen their representatives. Certain walls carry sham notices from "the Worshipful Company of Topers," from "all the Pompeians," and from a schoolmaster Valentius, who is made to write his recommendation in outrageously bad grammar (*Valentius cum discentes suos*).

These poor people were very human and in most ways very like ourselves. The scandals of the Imperial Court did not make much difference to a small provincial town. Three hundred years later we should have found a very different state of things. We should have found the middle class ruined by inflation and heavy taxation, the towns dwindling to mere forts, men bound by law to their father's occupation, and a general sense that civilization was doomed, as indeed it was.

The position of the slaves was probably better then than in the first century, and the Christian Church was teaching men and women to save their souls, though their country they could not save.

The causes of the decline and fall of Rome have

been differently estimated; perhaps the ruin of ancient civilization has never been fully accounted for. To some extent the Roman Empire died of Rome, an octopus which devoured everything and produced very little.

Hardly any of the inventions which have increased wealth and population so enormously in our time owe anything to Rome. In a slave state labour-saving is not worth while, and under the Empire the sciences made very little progress.

May, 1939.

VI

ARE GREAT MEN ALWAYS BAD?

"Power always corrupts. Absolute power corrupts absolutely. Great men are always bad."

These are the words of Lord Acton, Gladstone's friend, a prodigy of learning, whose ambition was to write a comprehensive history of freedom.

The last words must of course be taken in their context. Acton did not mean that St. Paul and Dante and Shakespeare were either not great or were bad. He was thinking of men like Julius Cæsar, Frederick the Great and Napoleon.

Shelley expresses the same conviction more hysterically. "Power, like a desolating pestilence, pollutes whate'er it touches." Shelley was an anarchist; Acton a Victorian Liberal. Both hated tyrants and dictators.

Acton thought that a historian ought to pass moral judgments. If he finds a historical character odious, he ought to say so.

He blamed Bishop Creighton, the historian of the Papacy, for his moral detachment. The bishop, he says, passes through scenes of raging crime and infamous treachery with serene indifference, a divided jury and a pair of white gloves. Even the Borgias get off easily in his history.

Creighton might have answered—most modern

historians would have agreed with him—that the historian is not a preacher of righteousness. He, however, answered more characteristically. "The good are not so good as they think themselves, and the bad are not so bad as the good think them."

I happen to have been reading some lives of typical great men who have used and abused power —Emil Ludwig and Madelin on Napoleon, Duff Cooper on Talleyrand, and Ludwig on Bismarck.

These are modern historians, whose idea of biography is to present us with the picture of a soul on its journey through life. Psychology necessarily brings us nearer to moral judgments than history as treated by Creighton.

It does not seem likely that any of the men who drew the highest prizes in life's lottery had any clear notion, in early life, of how far they were going. They were not cautious schemers, husbanding their resources. Julius Cæsar was a notorious profligate, who piled up enormous debts. Talleyrand's habits were a scandal even when ecclesiastics were not expected to believe in Christianity. Bismarck was a typical Junker, a duellist, a heavy drinker and gross eater, not even a hard worker. Napoleon could not afford these indulgences; he probably was consumed with ambition; but he could not have guessed what vast opportunities were about to be open to him.

It is very curious that Napoleon and Talleyrand, like Charles James Fox, both married women of bad character, who could be only a hindrance to their careers. Josephine's infidelities, both before and after her marriage to Napoleon, were notorious. Catherine Worlée and Bet Armistead were almost unblushingly professional.

Aristotle's definition of the "great-souled man" is that he thinks himself worthy of a great position and is worthy of it. All these men became gradually conscious that they were supremely competent, and that their rivals were not. Thereupon they pushed their way to the front without the slightest scruple.

Complete unscrupulousness is to be found in all of them. Lucan says of Julius Cæsar: "He says that laws were not made for him." "Men of my stamp," said Napoleon, "do not commit crimes."

Madame de Staël, a very shrewd woman, gives her early impression of Napoleon, then only General Bonaparte. "The dread with which this man fills me is a thing apart. He is neither good nor bad, neither gentle nor cruel. He can neither inspire nor feel affection; he is more and less than a man. He neither loves nor hates; he despises the nation whose applause he seeks. I have never been able to breathe freely in his presence."

This is the character of an Italian of the Renaissance. Bismarck was a typical German, with one German weakness—he was a vindictive hater. A statesman, if he knows his business, can afford few friends and no enemies.

Talleyrand had a far cooler judgment than either

of them. He said to Lamartine, "There are many
ways in which a statesman can be honest; my way
is not yours. But my pretended crimes are the
dreams of imbeciles. Has a clever man ever the
need to commit a crime? Crime is the resource of
political half-wits." He was accused of plotting
against and betraying every master whom he
served. His answer was plausible if not altogether
convincing. He deserted them all in turn, because
all in turn lost their heads and made themselves
impossible. He never intentionally gave them bad
advice, and he never betrayed France.

Nothing is more characteristic of him than his
death-bed conversion. "In truth," he said, "there
is nothing less aristocratic than unbelief." So he
made his reconciliation with the Church by repent-
ing—not of his fifty years of profligacy or his insatiable avarice—that was not required of him, but of
accepting the civil constitution of the clergy, and
of marrying his mistress.

He had moved with the times; in his young days
unbelief was not at all unaristocratic. But then he
had not been "absolutely corrupted by absolute
power," which he never possessed; intellectually
he had no illusions.

Napoleon, it is clear, lost all sense of what was
possible. He was, after all, a *condottiere* of genius,
with vulgar standards of success. Bismarck knew
where to stop—that was his greatness; but his
arrogance became insupportable, and his plan for

putting down Socialism by shooting the Socialists was absurd, as the young Kaiser rightly realized.

The degrees of comparison for an ambitious man are: "Get on. Get honour. Get honest." There is not always time for the superlative to take effect. If happiness is the object, the game is not worth the candle. Power, to judge by the confessions of those who have had it, does not make men happy. Most of the finer values of life have been sacrificed to the one great game. "God gave them their desire, and sent leanness withal into their souls." And what shall it profit a man, if he shall gain the whole world and lose his own soul?

And yet, if such men complain, as they always do, of the ingratitude of their contemporaries, have they not something to say for themselves? Napoleon could point to the restoration of order out of chaos in France, and to the famous *Code Napoléon*, the model of half the codes of the civilized world.

Bismarck could point to the German Empire, his creation; Julius Cæsar to the Roman Empire, which lasted for many centuries.

Revolutions are not made with rose-water, nor by scrupulous men. The life of a great man is generally a tragedy; but the tragic hero, as was said 2,000 years ago, is not a thoroughly bad man; if he fails, it is through some great error, an error, perhaps, which a smaller man would not make.

Stalin and Mussolini have already had a longer innings than Napoleon; and this much must be said in their favour, that neither they nor Hitler live in rampant vice and self-indulgence, like most of their predecessors.

Most of us dislike them, and what they seem to stand for; but we may remember Victor Hugo's remark in *Les Misérables*: "In order to be successful, it is not enough to be wicked."

January, 1939.

VII

THREE HUMAN MONSTERS

1. NERO

LAST year I wrote four essays on the greatest experiment in government by dictators—the Roman Empire. I chose Augustus, the model for all future dictators, Trajan, the Spanish officer, who ruled well and was rather oddly exempted by the Mediæval Church from the eternal punishment awarded to all other pagans, Marcus Aurelius, the pagan saint who failed to justify Plato's notion that kings should be philosophers or philosophers kings, and Julian, the pagan diehard, who could not read the signs of the times.

I am now going to describe three monsters of wickedness in high places, whose careers illustrate Lord Acton's saying that power always corrupts, and absolute power corrupts absolutely.

The hereditary principle was a failure at Rome. After Tiberius the world was ruled in succession by a madman, a pedant, and a monster. Nero was the monster. The succession was the weakest part of the Roman system; assassination was not always a satisfactory remedy.

The young Nero was only sixteen at his accession. Badly educated, he had none of the qualities of a ruler, unless it is to his credit that he was a fairly good musician and vocalist, and wrote tolerable verses.

"What an artist the world loses in me!" he exclaimed on the last day of his life, and he probably thought it.

For five years he was popular and well spoken of. He was guided by two remarkable men, Seneca and Burrus. Seneca, whom Carlyle unkindly called the father of all such as wear shovel hats, was a philosophic director or father confessor, whose works, too much neglected now, are full of noble exhortations and really splendid pulpit eloquence.

The Middle Ages believed that he was half a Christian, and that he corresponded with St. Paul. But like Cardinal Wolsey, whom he somewhat resembles, he made a prodigious fortune, and lived with a pomp unworthy of a philosopher. Like almost all others who lived at Nero's court, he paid for his elevation with his life.

When he reached man's estate, Nero abandoned himself to every vice and every crime. He murdered two wives, one of them by a brutal kick. He murdered his mother Agrippina, a wicked woman, whose ambition led her to many crimes. He poisoned his young relative Britannicus, the son of his predecessor. One after another, all the best men in Rome were struck down. Most of them anticipated their fate by opening their veins in a hot bath, a mode of suicide which is said not to be painful, but has gone out of fashion in favour of the gas oven.

Like the Mohawks and Apaches of the eighteenth century, he went about the streets at night in disguise, with his boon companions, assaulting passers-by.

His extravagance was as colossal as his criminality. In a few years he squandered £18,000,000. He spent £35,000 on Egyptian roses for a single banquet. His mules were shod with silver, and he never made a progress with less than a thousand carriages.

After the Great Fire of Rome, he covered a great part of the ruins with a palace of fabulous size and magnificence, known as the Golden House. The grounds included an artificial lake, where sham naval battles were fought.

These excesses, and private habits quite unmentionable, did not disgust the Romans so much as the appearance of the Emperor on the stage, which outraged their sense of dignity.

Why did they tolerate him for several years? Because there was no possible alternative form of government. The Senate still enjoyed great prestige, but no power. The senators were terrified and servile; they all lived, so to speak, with ropes round their necks. The tyranny was chiefly confined to Rome; the provinces were decently governed, whoever was emperor. And the mob were not terrorized like the aristocracy. They demonstrated against the Emperor, insulted and lampooned him. This is a curious feature of Roman despotism, which was continued at Constantinople. Justinian had reason to fear the riots in the Hippodrome.

In Church history Nero figures chiefly as the author of the first persecution of the Christians. There has been endless discussion as to whether he was the first to enact that the mere profession of Christianity was a capital offence.

The following is the account of Tacitus, who wrote about A.D. 120. Even at this date a Roman aristocrat disdained to know much about an obscure and unpopular sect. The Roman populace believed that the great fire was started by Nero himself, who was reported to have "fiddled while Rome was burning." Nothing is more unlikely, but scapegoats had to be found.

"To get rid of the report Nero fastened the guilt and inflicted the most exquisite tortures on a class hated for their abominations, whom the populace called Christians. Christ, after whom they were named, was executed in the reign of Tiberius by one of our procurators, Pontius Pilate.

"A mischievous superstition, checked for the moment, broke out again not only in Judea, but in Rome, where all ugly and shameful things become popular. . . . An immense multitude was convicted, not so much of the crime of firing the city, as of hatred towards mankind. Mockery of every sort was added to their deaths. Covered with the skins of beasts they were torn to death by dogs, or nailed to crosses, or burnt to serve as a nightly illumination. Even for such criminals there arose a feeling of compassion; for it was, it seemed, not for the public good, but to glut one man's cruelty, that they were being destroyed."

The "immense multitude" was probably only a few hundreds, and the story does not read like a systematic persecution. Was it Nero who gave the hint to Hitler to fire the Reichstag and throw the blame on the Communists?

We might have supposed that the assassination of this monster would have been hailed with universal satisfaction. But Nero was popular. His vulgar buffoonery hit the popular taste; his prodigality ministered to the pleasures of the mob. Above all, in him the sacred Julian line became extinct.

People refused to believe that he was dead. He had escaped to the East. Pretenders appeared again and again. Early in the second century Dion Chrysostom writes, "To the present time all men desire him to be alive, and the majority believe that he is alive."

In the Book of Revelation Nero is to return to lead the Parthians against Rome, which implies that he was not dead, or, alternatively, he is to come up from hell. Many have thought that the number of the Beast—666 or 616—is meant for "Nero Cæsar."

Why was he remembered, and why was he

regretted? His portraits show a coarse, brutal face, with a neck like a bull.

Nero may have had some redeeming qualities; Tacitus was not the man to record them if he had. But the evidence against him is too strong, he was, during the last years of his life, a monster of wickedness. And what is to be said of a system which may make such a man autocrat of the whole civilized world?

It is not only that the supreme power may, by ill luck fall into the hands of a demon, but that the possession of supreme power may turn a man who by nature is only weak, foolish and sensual into such a demon as history has agreed to represent the last of the Julian family to have been.

My next monster will be a man of a very different type, Timur the Tartar, who, without much meaning it, gave the moribund East Roman Empire fifty years more of life.

January, 1939.

In Northern Asia there is a vast zone of desert and steppe, stretching eastward from the Caspian. The surface consists of sand, salt steppes, gravel deserts and mountains, with cultivable soil near the rivers. In summer the temperature touches 120 in the shade, in winter falls to 30 degrees below zero.

The inhabitants can exist only in one way. They live on horseback, and sometimes cover 1,000 miles between their winter and summer pastures. The salt steppes during part of the year provide excellent grazing for sheep and horses.

The people must be content with the simplest utensils, which can be carried on the backs of camels; these used to include chains for their captives. The Tekke Turkomans carried off and held to ransom 1,000,000 Persians in the nineteenth century, till Skobeleff overthrew them in 1881.

Their wiry horses can carry their riders 100 miles a day. The Tartar cavalry could ride round any army, and they were unencumbered with transport, since they lived mainly on milk-products. They drank *kumiz*, fermented mares' milk. Their chief weapon was the lance—the Cossacks were armed Tartar-fashion to encounter them—but they were incomparable archers.

From time to time tribes of these mounted, mare-milking shepherds, forced out of the steppes by stronger neighbours, broke into Europe, and carried terror into civilized lands, for no army could withstand them. They are known in history as Scythians, Huns, Mongols and Tartars.

Their part in history has been thus summed up by an Austrian historian:

"Countries too distant from their base they could only ravage transitorily, with robbery, murder, fire and slavery; but the stamp which they left on the peoples whom they directly dominated remains ineffaceable. The East, the cradle and chief nursery of civilization, they delivered over to barbarism; they completely paralysed the greater part of Europe; they transformed and radically corrupted the race, spirit and character of countless millions for incalculable ages to come. That which is called the inferiority of the East European is their work, and if France and Germany had had steppes like Hungary, the light of Western civilization would probably long ago have been extinguished, the entire Old World would have been barbarized, and at the head of civilization would be stagnant China."

The most famous Mongolian conquerors have been Attila, in the fifth century, "the Scourge of God," who is commemorated in German folk-lore under the name of Etzel, Chinghiz or Genghiz Khan in the thirteenth century, and Timur the Tartar at the beginning of the fifteenth.

I have chosen the last partly because he is well known to readers of Christopher Marlowe under the name of Tamburlaine, and partly because of the romantic story of his war with the Turks, who, it must be remembered, were themselves originally a nomad tribe from Central Asia.

As experts in wholesale destruction there is not much to choose between them; but Timur, by destroying the Golden Horde, another Tartar tribe which had kept Russia in misery and barbarism for 200 years, made the recovery of Muscovy possible, and by annihilating the great Ottoman army at Angora gave Constantinople half a century more of independent life.

These were not exactly disinterested acts of benevolence. His favourite practice of marking the sites of flourishing cities by pyramids of the skulls of their inhabitants does not stamp him as a humanitarian.

This savage who aimed at the conquest of the world was an elderly cripple, a scientific chess-player and something of a theologian. Delhi and Samarkand, Bagdad, Aleppo and Damascus had already fallen to the attacks of his invincible cavalry, when he heard, on the banks of the Ganges, that the Ottoman Sultan, Bayazid or Bajazet, was preparing to resist him.

Sultan Bayazid was following up the conquests of his father, Murad, who had taken Salonica and Adrianople from the Greeks and had routed a powerful Balkan League at Kossovo. The Western Powers, alarmed at last, sent a great crusading army against the Turks; it was destroyed at Nicopolis in 1396.

Timur curtly ordered the great Sultan to restore his conquests to the Greeks. Transported with rage, Bayazid replied in a letter garnished with the choicest Oriental insults.

The two barbarians advanced to meet each other, each at the head of an enormous army. The scene of the battle was Angora, now the capital city of the late Kemal Ataturk. The Turkish host, against which no European army could stand, was destroyed, and the Sultan was taken prisoner.

When the Tartars approached Brusa, then the Turkish capital, the terrified inhabitants sent out their children to meet them, singing Mohammedan hymns. The Tartars rode over the children and massacred the whole population of Brusa. The narrow stream of the Bosphorus and Dardanelles saved Europe; the master of half a million horsemen could not beg, borrow or steal a single galley. Timur returned to Central Asia, and was planning the conquest of China when death overtook him.

His descendants, under the name of the great Moguls, ruled over part of India till the Mutiny.

The rapid recovery of the Turks from this overwhelming defeat seems to show that even Tartar destructiveness seldom alters the course of history permanently. For Constantinople fell fifty years later. The Huns invaded France under Attila in the fifth century, and by destroying the great Roman frontier fortress of Aquileia drove to the lagoons the refugees who afterwards founded Venice.

Both the Huns and Mongols only ruined countries where they were permanent masters, and not always even then. Russia suffered irreparable injury from the Golden Horde; under Scandinavian leadership they had made promising steps towards civilization.

Civilization, according to Peisker, the historian I have quoted, had a narrow escape. Is there any danger that it may some day be threatened again in a similar way? The mounted archer ceased to be formidable when gunpowder was discovered, and civilization seems now to be adequately protected against barbarian inroads. But if we ask whether wars of extermination, or of wholesale deportation with confiscation of land and property, are any longer possible, we cannot answer with as much confidence as we might have done in the last century.

If moral considerations are wholly disregarded, as they are openly in totalitarian States, this is the only kind of war which pays, assuming that the stronger nation desires more territory and has a surplus population to export. This seems to be the intention of the infamous persecution of the Jews in Germany, and this was the policy of the Turks in western Asia Minor, when over a million Greeks were driven out of the country, besides the very large number who were killed.

There have been several examples in history of the extirpation of indigenous populations. The Spaniards totally exterminated the Guanches of the Canary Islands and the Caribs of the Greater Antilles. The Indians in what is now the United States were destroyed over a great part of the continent. There are no Tasmanians left, except a few families of half-breeds on the islands between Tasmania and Australia.

Perhaps we cannot regard the destruction of savages by civilized men as quite so heinous a crime as, for instance, the annihilation by the Mongols of the interesting civilization of the Arabian Nights at Bagdad or the burning of Moscow by the Golden Horde. But is there any security that a strong, civilized State may not treat a weaker civilized State in the same way?

If there is no such thing as absolute right and wrong; if "reasons of State" justify any crime, we are back in the jungle, and another Attila or Timur may arise to scourge humanity. One of the old Scandinavian Eddas prophesies: "Wind Time! Wolf Time! There shall come a year, When no man on earth His brother man shall spare."

January, 1939.

3. IVAN THE TERRIBLE

Is Russia part of Europe or of Asia? The question
has often been discussed. Geographically, European
Russia is part of the Asiatic land mass, from which
the peninsula of Europe projects. The population is
mainly of European type, though the 200 years of
Tartar domination have given some justification
for the saying that if you scratch a Russian you find
a Tartar.

In culture, till Peter the Great, the nation was
entirely barbarous. There was no education;
illiteracy was almost universal, and so was bestial
drunkenness, which is not an Asiatic vice.

The House of Rurik, originally Swedish, ruled
over part of the vast plain as Grand Dukes of
Muscovy, till Dmitri, the son of Ivan the Terrible,
was murdered, and the Romanoffs began their
tragic career. Ivan was the first to call himself Tsar;
it meant that Russia, with the Byzantine two-
headed eagle as its totem, was the heir of the East
Roman Empire.

The reverence paid to the autocrat was quite
Oriental. The worst rulers were never removed.
Stephen Graham, Ivan's biographer, says: "The
Russians, passive to fate, have always proved piti-
fully incapable of assassinating those who oppressed
them. The belligerent, cruel, vigorous Ivan was

safer than an idealist would have been. Slaves and Slavs require a tyrant to rule over them."

Ivan ascended the throne as a child, and was still a boy when he married a good wife, who kept him fairly straight for several years. He was, and remained to the end, deeply religious, or rather grossly superstitious. He more than once thought of abdicating and becoming a monk. Death overtook him before he could execute his design, but his dead body was habited in a monk's cassock and renamed Johan.

Russian Christianity, however, was a queer thing. "To shave the beard," said Ivan, "is a sin that the blood of all the martyrs cannot cleanse. It is to deface the image of God." Peter the Great ordered his subjects to cut off their beards; many of them preferred to die.

When his wife, to whom he was really attached, died, Ivan went mad; he became a homicidal maniac. His portrait by Vasnetsof shows him carrying his favourite staff, with a spike at one end and a knob at the other. With the spike he would transfix the foot of a man who was brought before him; with the knob he broke men's heads in his frequent rages. At last he clubbed his eldest son, who died in consequence. This really horrified him, for a time.

One of his ambitions was to marry Queen Elizabeth. He gave great privileges to English merchants, and made formal proposals for the hand of the

Queen. Elizabeth, who was anxious not to lose the lucrative Russian trade, pretended to be flattered, and dallied with the proposal. But she rather spoilt the effect by sending the Tsar a cheap silver cup, and telling him that if his subjects ever got tired of him she would allow him to live in England "at his own charges." Good Queen Bess had a frugal mind.

Afterwards he wished to marry Lady Mary Hastings, the Queen's niece. The English made a joke of it, and called the lady "the Empress."

It would be tedious and unpleasant to describe the deeds which earned Ivan his nickname. By his orders thousands of people were impaled, roasted, boiled, flayed, racked to death, torn to pieces by bears, or beaten to death with the knout, a kind of flail with a heavy lash cut into three sharp edges. Torture was the Tsar's hobby, and not his only. The children of the gentry were allowed to look on as a treat.

On one occasion he massacred, with every refinement of cruelty, nearly the whole population of Novgorod. While the slaughter was going on he spent five days praying in a monastery. But soon he could not resist the pleasure of watching the sport. A thousand inhabitants of Novgorod were tortured to death each day in his presence and that of his son. Eye-witnesses estimated the number of victims at 27,000.

His other habits cannot be described. Stephen Graham gingerly lifts the cloak from one corner of the unutterable when he says that father and son periodically exchanged wives.

This Ivan was probably the greatest monster in human shape who ever disgraced humanity. There was not a single redeeming feature in his character. But when after murdering the Tsarevitch, the son of the only woman he ever loved, he proposed to abdicate, his subjects begged him to continue to rule over them for the term of his natural life.

He was insane, of course. But are we quite sure that we should not become rather queer if we had absolute power, with no one to contradict or resist or blame us, whatever we did?

The character of the tyrant has been drawn once for all by Plato, who is emphatic that tyranny is the worst of all forms of government, worse even than democracy, which Plato did not love. One or two of the petty Italian despots in the Middle Ages were almost as cruel as Ivan the Terrible.

Given a homicidal and sadistic maniac with absolute power, and subjects who are too fatalistic to get rid of him, we must expect to hear of strange things. But there is one question which is of more general interest. How is it that a bloodthirsty tyrant can always find, without difficulty, instruments to carry out his crimes? How is it that he can always enlist the services of spies, informers, perjurers, corrupt judges, gaolers, torturers and executioners?

We may be answered that Russia was not a

civilized country, and that the sixteenth century was not like the twentieth? I should have been content with this answer thirty years ago, but I cannot be content with it now. I used to think that, though in some ways we were no better than our ancestors, we were, at any rate, more humane.

But what do we see now? Do my readers know what is going on every day in the prison camps of Germany and Russia? Do they know that torture has been reintroduced into Europe? Do they know that from 4,000,000 to 6,000,000 peasants were deliberately allowed to die of hunger in Southern Russia five years ago because they were recalcitrant over Stalin's scheme of collectivization? Do they know that a hundred thousand innocent people were butchered by the Reds in Madrid alone in 1936?

Who carried out these orders? How comes it that Germany and Russia are so full of spies and informers that no one dares to speak freely? How are the savage secret police recruited? Would anyone who travelled in Germany or Spain or Russia before the troubles have thought so badly of the inhabitants? Can we say with confidence, "It can't happen here"? These are not pleasant thoughts. Is our civilization only skin-deep?

I do not really think that Europe is reverting to savagery, but it looks by no means so impossible as it did thirty years ago. The autocrat often becomes a fiend because he is above public opinion. We are all kept straight by public opinion, and if the rising generation rejects all traditional rules of right and wrong, despising them as antiquated taboos, we are likely to see some strange aberrations of conduct.

War and revolution have loosened all old ties; men and women are everywhere asking, "Why shouldn't I?" It is a deadly question, for the passions grant dispensations more readily than the most accommodating director of souls, and those who have grown accustomed to witness or take part in acts of cruelty soon become quite callous, and often take a morbid pleasure in inflicting pain.

January, 1939.

SOCIAL PROBLEMS

I

BOREDOM

MR. WINGFIELD STRATFORD, in his lively and
stimulating social history of Victorian England,
lets fall a remark which is worthy of the attention
of historians: "The influence of boredom on the
course of history has never been sufficiently allowed
for." Nations never know when they are well off.
They cannot stand being well governed for more
than a few years.

The author thinks that the Western Roman
Empire died of boredom, not of the Goths. But
there are several better examples. Louis Philippe,
with his umbrella and his *bourgeois* appearance, was
not a romantic figure. But has France ever been
better governed than during his reign? Nevertheless, as was said at the time, "France is bored."
So the old king was packed off in a four-wheeler.
"Fils de Saint Louis, montez au fiacre," as an unkind
bystander remarked.

France preferred Napoleon the Little, as Victor
Hugo called him, who gave her eighteen years of
shoddy magnificence, ending with Mexico and
Sedan.

Or take our own history. We did not recover
from the Napoleonic War till 1850. A series of

financial crises and "the hungry forties" made that period as unpleasant as that in which we are now living. But with 1850 began a time of unexampled prosperity and contentment. What did we do? We must needs pick a quarrel with Russia, which had not the slightest wish to attack us. Ministers were rushed into the Crimean War, which no one now defends, by popular enthusiasm. The people, or those who then had votes, were spoiling for a fight. It was not enough to force opium on the poor Chinese, who were too weak to make war amusing.

Even now there are people who would welcome war as a relief from humdrum existence. We old folk cannot understand this state of mind, but it exists. Wars always begin with a ringing of bells, and end with a wringing of hands. What a strange thing it is that in all the belligerent countries the suicide rate fell during the Great War! The drama was too exciting for the spectators to wish to walk out in the middle of it.

Makers of Utopias (the writing of these books is a masculine weakness; women never write them) always picture a static society, in which, perfection having been reached, there is no need for further change. They do not allow for the frantic boredom which would soon produce a violent rebellion.

There are static societies, no doubt—those of the social insects. But we may hope that the bees and ants are mercifully in ignorance of the purgatory in which they live. If we had the virtues of the little busy bee, and of the ant which is an example to the sluggard, we should not be the lords of creation, nor should we be so discontented.

Could we endure to live in a Fabian farmyard of tame animals? We should be bored stiff, and be ready for any "reaction," even a military dictator who would chastise us with scorpions.

There is an amusing paragraph in which William James describes how he spent a few days in a sort of summer camp, exposed to the full force of moral and spiritual uplift. "Ouf! What a relief!" he exclaimed when he escaped. He missed, he confesses, "the dear old Devil." A little girl once said, "Mummy, if I am very good in Heaven, shall I sometimes be allowed to have a little devil up to play with?" She agreed with William James.

The mere fact of security is enough to drive many people mad with impatience and boredom. The privileged oligarchs under the four Georges used to gamble away their fortunes, like the last Marquess of Hastings, one of the richest men in England, who is said to have lost £140,000 in one day, and died, a broken man, at twenty-six, or the notorious madcap, Jack Mytton, of Shropshire. Even now rich men often perform foolhardy exploits, as if life without danger were not worth living.

The question of boredom affects not only politics and life in society, but science, philosophy and religion. It is well known that our most popular teachers in astronomy and physics, men like Jeans and Eddington, are convinced that the universe is slowly running down like a clock. It will have an end, when life will be extinct everywhere; and therefore it must have had a beginning. Since they know of no recuperative process in Nature, it must have started "with a bang," as Eddington says. This sounds very orthodox; we used to be told that the bang took place in 4004 B.C., but it is a queer doctrine for a man of science. The theory favoured in antiquity, and by some even to-day, is that as perpetuity is the time-form of eternity, so recurrence, in vast cosmic cycles, is the time-form of the activity of an unchanging Creator. If the universe is running down like a clock, it must have been wound up like a clock, and it seems reasonable to suppose that whatever power wound it up once will probably wind it up again. But our pundits are manifestly prejudiced against the idea of recurrence. Jeans has to admit that the shrunken stars, the "white dwarfs," may go on indefinitely in their present state. "It is difficult to see with what object," he adds. Another odd remark from a mathematician! Others reject the theory of recurrence as "extreme pessimism." But is this poor old earth such a very bad place to live in? To me it is rather a comfort to know that our Utopian reformers cannot do very much mischief with all their efforts. If we adopt the theory of recurrence, we must give up Tennyson's "one increasing purpose." I do not know what an increasing purpose means; but it is obvious that an eternal purpose is eternally frustrate, for a purpose fulfilled is no longer a purpose.

The problem really boils down to this. Would the Creator be bored by administering a static universe? Can we imagine Him playing an infinite series of games of patience by Himself? Are Christian theology and philosophy right in teaching that God never changes, never develops into anything that He was not before?

And we ourselves, are we to look forward to a state of unchanging fruition, which is the orthodox Christian view, or with Tennyson should we pray: "Give us the wages of going on and not to die"? Is not the prospect of the Christian Heaven, to speak very frankly, intolerably boring? Especially if we happen not to be musical, is not the prospect of having to listen through all eternity to interminable performances of orchestral music almost enough to deter us from the practice of virtue?

The idea of progress in Heaven is no part of the Christian religion, which does not mean that it is necessarily false. But the whole difficulty, it seems to me, is caused by our habit of regarding eternal life simply as a series of moments of time, snipped off at one end—at the moment when we are "launched into eternity" by the hangman's rope or in the course of Nature, but not at the other.

We can hardly help translating eternity into the language of time and place, but if we take these word-pictures literally we shall think salvation terribly boring, and reprobation senselessly cruel.

When we die, whatever our fate may be, we have probably done with time altogether, unless we believe in reincarnation, an idea which is firmly believed by most Asiatics, and by more people in Europe than is generally realized. And where there is no time, there can be no boredom. Nor do we ever get tired of the purest pleasures, which raise us into a timeless state here on earth.

Schopenhauer said that the two foes of happiness are pain and boredom, and that in the degree in which we escape one we approach the other. This is real pessimism. If we are bored with ourselves, it is because we have chosen a dull companion with no high interests; but this is curable.

February, 1939.

II

ALIEN IMMIGRANTS

I HAVE said, in writing about the Jews, that the German political slogan of race and blood is unscientific balderdash, since there are no pure races. Even the Jews, who have been estranged from their neighbours in their adopted countries by religion and by persecution, are very much mixed, and the Germans are not even predominantly Nordic.

The greatest advances in civilization have been made by the fusion of two cultures. The ancient Greeks are one example; the Christian Church is another.

Opinions differ as to whether mixed marriages are desirable. The children often start with a disadvantage, like the Eurasians (now rather absurdly called Anglo-Indians) in India, and the mulattoes in North America. On the other hand, the beauty of the quadroons (one-quarter negro) used to be celebrated, and some experts speak of "hybrid vigour." The theory is that for one or two generations the offspring of miscegenation is more energetic than either of the parents.

The general opinion is that while the eugenist would look with approval on the marriage of an Englishman and an Italian, or a German and a Jew, the mixture of two very different racial types, such as the European and the negro, Mongolian, or aboriginal Australian, should not be encouraged.

The most extraordinary melting pot in the world is Hawaii, where the natives of the Sandwich Islands mate with whites of every nation, and with Chinese and Japanese. The results, judging from photographs, are decidedly pleasing; but the Polynesians, wherever they came from, are not very unlike Europeans.

The children of white New Zealanders and Maoris are splendid men physically, as we saw when a team of athletes, most of them half-breeds, visited this country.

But the refugees whom we have always welcomed to our shores have belonged to kindred stocks, and if we can find room for them there is not the smallest reason why we should not receive them. Even the Jews, who are sometimes, by no means always, recognizable as aliens, make good citizens. They seldom come on the rates, and many of them have won distinction in science, literature and administration, as well as in commerce.

Our island has been successfully invaded again and again. The Celts, who, contrary to the usual opinion, were akin to the Teutons, mingled with the dark "Mediterranean" people whom they found in possession. The Romans left very few traces of Italian blood. The Roman armies under the empire were not made up of Italians; the legions quartered in Britain sometimes came from Spain; the men doubtless took British wives.

The Saxon and Danish conquests were a very different affair; there was a real displacement of population; probably the majority of the Britons were killed or driven off by the English, who in their turn had reason to pray, "From the fury of the Northmen, good Lord deliver us."

The Normans, a blend of Scandinavians and Gauls, were a very fine race, but William's army brought very few women, and the "Norman blood" of which Tennyson speaks was very much diluted.

Since then there has been no hostile immigration, though some Cornishmen, oddly enough, like tc imagine that the shipwrecked sailors of the Spanish Armada found favour with Cornish girls. In point of fact, they were given no opportunity of displaying their seductive manners.

But there has been friendly immigration on a fairly large scale, and we have profited greatly by it. Henry I imported colonies of Flemish weavers, who taught our people to make the coarse woollen cloth called frieze, and Edward III brought in more of them. Honesty compels me to add that in 1381 the mob who murdered the Archbishop of Canterbury and sacked John of Gaunt's London palace, massacred all the Flemish weavers whom they could find.

The great influx of French Huguenots after the revocation of the Edict of Nantes is well known.

Men who are willing to go into banishment for their religious opinions are likely to have unusual strength of character, and there can be no doubt that Louis XIV expelled some of the best of his subjects. Books have been written about the after-history of the Huguenot families. It is an astonishing record.

The only parallel that I know is the history of the descendants of the Pilgrim Fathers in the United States. A large percentage of the most distinguished Americans trace their descent from the pilgrims on the *Mayflower*, though some scepticism is perhaps justified. The *Mayflower* was not quite as large as the *Mauretania*.

Well, we are now welcoming a large number of refugees from Germany, and a smaller number from Russia. Hitler is imitating our Edward I, who, after encouraging the Jews to lend money at staggering rates of interest, bled them white by every kind of cruelty and then banished them. Cromwell brought them back; but as late as 1753 there was a savage outbreak of anti-Semitism in England.

The victims of Hitler's persecution seem to be mainly intellectuals. There are said to be over 300 foreign scientists now in the British Empire, most of them in England. Five of them are Nobel Prizemen for science.

Care must be taken not to reveal the identity of these eminent men, some of whom probably have relatives who might come under the lash of the secret police in Germany. But it is said that they include at least one leader in cancer research, and one who helped Germany during the Great War by discovering how to extract nitrogen from the atmosphere. Another, not a German, I think, has studied the migrations of fish. Another has advanced the processes of making synthetic rubber and sugar. Another is associated with the new discovery of "heavy water," from which great things are expected by scientific chemists.

Such a galaxy of imported talent ought to give our country the first place in experimental science. That these men are grateful to their hosts, and eager to do their best for the country that has welcomed them, need not be doubted. The greatest of them all, Einstein, has found refuge in America.

Is there such a thing as collective insanity? I am utterly bewildered by the orgy of callous cruelty and senseless persecution which has broken out since the Great War, in Russia, Spain, Germany and other countries. I must leave it to wiser men to find a rational explanation of it all; I do not understand it.

At any rate there is no doubt about the facts. The horrors that are going on are worse than anything that has appeared in print. Innocent people are being murdered every day by the secret police, and torture is regularly applied in the concentration camps. The relief of the poor victims who have escaped from this inferno is piteous to see.

Can we say that such a state of things is too bad to

last? The average citizen of a totalitarian state is a decent enough fellow, certainly not a cruel monster. True enough; but he cannot call his soul his own. There is no escape from modern tyranny.

The fatal objection to State Socialism or State Capitalism (they are the same thing) is that it makes the government omnipotent. Every man's life, liberty and livelihood are at the mercy of some official. As Herbert Spencer said, "Socialism will mean slavery, and the slavery will not be mild." The government may or may not wish to relax the reign of terror, but it does not dare to do it.

As the Chinese proverb says, "He who rides on a tiger can never dismount." Many Germans, alas! are wishing for war as their only chance of deliverance.

March, 1939.

III

QUEER TABOOS

THE word "taboo," or *tabu*, was introduced into
English by Captain Cook, who met with it at
Tonga in the Pacific. It means something which
must not be done—no questions asked. The savage
lives in terror of violating a taboo. A stalwart Maori
died of horror after eating some food reserved for his
chief, though the chief did not mind.

But the superstition is not peculiar to savages.
One of the strangest things in the history of religion
is that almost all religions make certain rules which
cannot seriously be regarded as coming under the
head of moral conduct, but which nevertheless have
to be observed as strictly as what our Lord called the
weightier matters of the law.

It is easy to see that such rules must blunt the
moral sense of those who have to keep them. If we
think that our Maker is as much offended with us for
drinking a glass of beer or smoking a pipe or eating
a mutton chop on Friday as for telling a lie or nurs-
ing a grudge against our neighbour, we must give up
regulating our conduct by our innate sense of right
and wrong. We must surrender the right and the
duty of private judgment.

In the Gospels there are no rules of this kind, and

we gather that in the opinion of our Lord there ought to be none. He performed works of mercy on the Sabbath, and in one ancient manuscript of St. Luke He is reported to have said to a man whom He found working on the Sabbath, "Man, if thou knowest what thou doest thou art blessed, but if thou knowest not thou art cursed and a transgressor of the law."

This was too strong meat for the early Church, and the story disappeared from the Canon. But He had no patience with the "Touch not, taste not, handle not" of Jewish tradition. Christianity was to be a religion without irrational taboos.

Modern Jews, as far as I have observed, pay very little attention to these traditions of the elders, though there is a good story of Cardinal Vaughan asking the Chief Rabbi when they would see him eating ham, to which the Cardinal had helped himself. "At your Eminence's wedding," answered the Chief Rabbi.

The survival value of taboos is extraordinary. A certain tribe, which had been converted to Christianity, was cut off from all communication with Christian bodies for centuries. When they were re-discovered every trace of Christian belief had vanished, but two customs survived. They fasted in Lent, and made the sign of the Cross.

Taboos are useful as outward signs of membership in a religious body. We ought, perhaps, to be able to point to something which we do or leave undone simply out of loyalty. At any rate, this motive is strong among many religious people.

In spite of the plain intention of the Founder to impose no obligations except moral ones, Christianity has enforced as many taboos as any other religion. The New Testament already knows of sectarians who "forbid to marry," and before long we find Fathers of the Church speaking of the axe of virginity cutting down the tree of marriage.

For centuries this kind of total abstinence was a test of the highest virtue. In some branches of the Church it is still taught that virginity is a higher state than marriage. Society under paganism had been very corrupt, and it may be argued that it was worth while to prove that this kind of self-denial is possible. The pagans, in point of fact, were much impressed by it. The physician Galen says that in this particular the Christians are "not inferior to real philosophers."

Apart from this counsel of perfection, the Catholics have always insisted on certain well-known dietary rules, which are also observed by many Anglicans. To a Protestant these rules are not obligatory, but some kind of self-denial in eating and drinking is good for most people. What is not respectable is sham fasting, elaborately cooked fish dinners and so forth.

Protestant taboos are very numerous. Campaigns against alcohol might be justified when drunkenness was a national vice, as it was very notably in the eighteenth century, when gentlemen were not ashamed to be intoxicated and the populace was soaked in gin. But in England, and still more in America, teetotal fanatics have made themselves ridiculous and objectionable.

I remember visiting America at the time when the great Republic was supposed to be bone dry. Before I landed I found myself surrounded by reporters in the saloon of the *Mauretania*. "Well, Dr. Inge," they said, "what is your opinion of Prohibition?" I said that I was quite willing to be an abstainer for three weeks; "but, since you ask me, I think that cold water, with which the wild asses quench their thirst, is a poor beverage to offer to a human being." Needless to say, this appeared in all the papers next day.

There are, or were then, some States of the Union in which it was unsafe to smoke in public, unless one wished to be called a cigarette fiend. This was a genuine religious taboo. "Worship the Lord with clean lips," was the text on which they relied. This rule is not unknown among English Nonconformists, and it was strictly enforced by the Mohammedan sect of Wahhabis.

Attempts have been made in the United States to put down tea-drinking. It is not generally known that the outbreak at Boston which began the American War of Independence, when chests of tea were thrown into the harbour, was not exactly political. The placards at Boston complained, not that the English want to tax us without our consent, but that they want to poison us with their noxious drugs. The Americans have now partially succumbed to tea, but they still keep up a taboo against mustard.

The old Evangelicalism is so much a matter of past history that only old people remember the formidable list of Puritan taboos. It was quite unjustifiable to identify the Christian Sunday with the Jewish Sabbath and then to burden the Christian Sunday with a number of prohibitions which might have pleased the Pharisees, but which very few Jews now take seriously.

Secular books must not be read; no exercise must be taken except a quiet walk in the afternoon. Some old-fashioned people regret the loss of what was certainly a day of rest; but the Puritan Sunday was much more Jewish than Christian.

Tunbridge Wells, a citadel of Evangelicalism, had no theatre when I was a boy; theatre-going and card-playing were tabooed by strict Christians; and I can remember a taboo upon "yellow-backed novels." This was a survival of an old idea that novels are not true, and therefore are objectionable.

Taboo-morality is now out of fashion. But there is grave danger of "emptying out the baby with the bath-water." The question, Why shouldn't I? has ruined many lives. Some of these prohibitions are not so absurd as they appear. They represent the stored experience of the race.

Religion, the most conservative instinct in the world, preserves many antiquated absurdities, petrified fossils of thought and practice; but it also preserves many valuable traditions, without which civilization would be in danger. The most stable, though not the most progressive, societies in the world are those which are content to live by consecrated custom.

There is one Puritan taboo which I should much like to revive—that against all betting and gambling. Drunkenness is no longer a national vice; betting is. I shall never forget what a prison chaplain said to me when I asked him what class of malefactors he found the least hopeful. He answered, "Those who have come to prison as the result of betting and gambling."

March, 1939.

CRIME AND PUNISHMENT

THE proposed changes in our criminal law have revived the familiar and interminable debates about the ethics of punishment and the efficacy of our methods of dealing with criminals.

Sir Arthur Greer, than whom there is no higher authority, enumerates the aims of punishment as (1) to satisfy public indignation; (2) to deter the criminal from repeating his crime; (3) to deter others from doing the same. He thinks there is a real danger of making prison too comfortable.

On such questions we must listen to those who have had experience in administering the law. But a few considerations may be offered by an outsider.

Imprisonment is a highly unjust penalty, because to some it brings shame more dreaded than death, while to others it brings no felt disgrace and not much discomfort. This is proved by the existence of a class of professional criminals who are willing again and again to incur the risk of detection.

Public opinion is ready to inflict the maximum of moral cruelty, while it shrinks from even the minimum of physical cruelty. It is quite right to break the neck of a murderer instead of strangling him in the old way, for intending suicides who have been cut down just in time have testified that death by strangulation is horribly painful; but what is five minutes of suffering compared with the prolonged misery of the victim of a sensational murder trial?

I am not in favour of abolishing capital punishment, nor do I understand why it is objected to. The State has as good a right to remove an incorrigible public enemy as a gardener has to pull up weeds in his garden. The old argument that the Book of Genesis sanctions the execution of murderers but of no others is absurd on several grounds. The legislation of the Hebrews, in point of fact, imposed the death penalty for other offences, such as adultery and even Sabbath-breaking.

But the capital sentence ought to be simply the removal of a public nuisance, not an act of public vengeance. It should be carried out privately, in a lethal chamber, or an electric chair as in America, and without any unnecessary humiliation. The condemned man should be encouraged to carry out the sentence on himself.

It is sometimes said that capital punishment is no deterrent. This is quite contrary to experience. In Italy, where there are practically no executions except under military law, there are more than ten times as many murders as in England. The United States, where executions are comparatively rare, has a pre-eminence in homicide. When the abolition of the capital penalty was proposed in France, a witty Frenchman said, "Henceforth the law in

France will guarantee the lives of none except murderers."

The same exaggerated sensibility about inflicting physical violence is seen in the agitation, which will probably be successful, against corporal punishment. This is a more difficult question.

The Jews, as we may see from the Books of Proverbs and Ecclesiasticus, had a strong belief in the remedial value of "stripes." The flogging schoolmaster, from Horace's Orbilius to Dr. Keate of Eton, wielded his weapons without protest down to our own day. The most savage floggings in the Army and Navy went on till almost within living memory, and in the eighteenth century poor Magdalenes were whipped at Newgate "till their backs were bloody," in the presence of gentlemen who came to see the sport.

Modern psychology has brought to light the connection of flagellation with the disorders of sex called "sadism" and "masochism," and this ugly association has led many to think that corporal punishment should be abolished altogether. On the other hand, physical pain, the fear of which is certainly a deterrent, may be considered the most appropriate punishment for brutal assaults and wanton cruelty. Habitual criminals are said to dislike the birch more than the cat, because this ignominious punishment makes them laughed at by their mates.

Many experiments have been tried, especially in

the United States, in substituting State reformatories, in which those who are detained are called inmates, not prisoners, for imprisonment. The general opinion seems to be that the results are good with first offenders, but that they are usually ineffective with habitual criminals.

It is generally admitted that extreme severity, such as existed in England till the reforms advocated by Romilly and others after the Napoleonic War, is a mistake from every point of view. About 100 offences were legally punishable with death, and the death sentence was freely pronounced, though not often carried out.

In 1830 there were 50,000 convicts in England, though the population was then only fifteen millions. One judge, however, justified the system as giving a great discretion to the judge, who might occasionally allow the sentence to be carried out, thus ridding society of an incorrigible rogue.

In all early societies some sins are punished as crimes. The plea that "the gods should be left to deal with offences against themselves" was not favoured. Certain offences were supposed to bring down the wrath of heaven, not only on the culprits, but on the tribe or city.

This belief or superstition had a great effect on criminal law. The suicide was buried at the crossroads with a stake through his body, to prevent his ghost from walking. The fate of Sodom and Gomorrah justified the State in hanging those whose morals resembled those of the Cities of the Plain. I remember reading in an old law-book: "*Sacrilege. Stealing anything from a church. Penalty, transportation for life. Note: this does not apply to thefts from the chapels of dissenters, for which see Petty Larceny.*"

The distinction between sin and crime ought to be more carefully observed. As a Christian, I should almost always try to dissuade a man from declaring his innings closed; but suicide is not a crime. I believe it is not a crime in any other European country.

Abnormal proclivities are often more like disease than crime; the main duty of the criminal law here is to protect boys and girls, and to safeguard public decency.

The law of high treason ought certainly to be made applicable to political strikes, like that of 1926.

As for the moral question, popular in debating societies, about the right to punish, very few will agree with Tolstoy that the State has no such right. But there will always be some who argue that punishment must always be remedial in intention, not vindictive, and others who argue that it is immoral to punish a man for any other reason than because his acts deserve it.

Presumably, moral indignation was given us to be used, but it is odd what very different acts have aroused it in different ages. In the Middle Ages the heretic and the traitor were the persons whom almost everyone wished to see burnt alive, or hanged, drawn and quartered. Now cruelty, which hardly appears as a deadly sin in the old catalogues, is the crime for which there is no forgiveness.

As for remedial punishment, it ought not to be called punishment at all, any more than a surgical operation, which may incidentally be painful. Mr. Nosnibor, in Butler's *Erewhon*, was ordered several floggings by his "straightener" to cure him of his propensity to embezzle money; but this was a prescription, not a punishment. His friends called next day to inquire how he was after his flogging.

December, 1938.

V

HAVELOCK ELLIS

I NEVER met Havelock Ellis, who died recently. I once tried to make his acquaintance, but he civilly intimated that he was rather shy of parsons. His books fill nearly a shelf of my library; I have them all, with one exception. The exception is his great work on the *Psychology of Sex*, in six volumes. This is the book which was not allowed to be published in England; it was banned as obscene literature, and a bookseller was prosecuted for selling a copy.

The friends of Ellis were naturally indignant at such an insult to an eminent man of science, the last man in the world to corrupt public morals or to enjoy plying the muck-rake. As in other well-known cases of more recent date, the censorship was roundly abused and held up to scorn.

The case, however, was not so simple as that. There are classes of men—medical specialists, judges, magistrates, priests and schoolmasters—whose business it is to know the depths of human depravity and the aberrations (sometimes a matter for the pathologist rather than for the criminal courts) to which the human mind is liable. It is admitted that Ellis's book contained much valuable information of this kind. But it does not follow that cold-blooded descriptions of beastliness should be sold over the counter to anyone who can pay for them.

As a classical scholar, I have several books on my shelves which would be confiscated by the police if they were written in English instead of in Greek or Latin. I do not think they do me any harm. But I must confess that I burnt the first two volumes of the *Psychology of Sex* as being too unwholesome. An abridged edition, with much less offensive matter, is now procurable.

However, this is no reproach to Ellis, whose book helped to promote a more rational attitude to abnormalities which for many centuries had been ferociously punished as crimes. Superstition and the story of the fate of Sodom and Gomorrah had something to do with the horror which vented itself in extreme severity.

In the sixteenth century a cock was condemned to be burnt alive for the unnatural offence of laying an egg. Only a few years ago a man was sentenced to eighteen months' imprisonment with hard labour for dressing as a woman, and the sentence was upheld on appeal. Alienists know that this is a recognized form of mental eccentricity, not generally associated with immoral conduct.

One of Ellis's earlier books is called *The Task of Social Hygiene*. Social hygiene, he says, is more radical and more scientific than social reform. It must complete the work which the reforms of the nineteenth century began. Social reform accepts the stream of life as it finds it, and while working to cleanse the banks of the stream makes no attempt to purify the stream itself.

We may mark four stages in the movement of the nineteenth century. First came the effort to make our towns clean and sanitary. Then factory legislation. Then education, and lastly the effort to guard the child before school age, and to bestow due care on the future mother. All these are environmental; there can be no radical cure of social evils until the State acknowledges its responsibility for the intrinsic quality of its citizens.

This means of course that Ellis was an enthusiastic eugenist. He was an early disciple of that great man, Sir Francis Galton, and, like his master, realized that it is useless to try to legislate in advance of public opinion. Ellis however is much less cautious than Galton, who was always moderate, almost conservative. But he accepted the view that the task of the eugenist is to educate public opinion. It is a slow and disheartening labour. In some ways there has been a distinct falling back since Ellis's earlier books. In fact, the whole trend of thought since the Great War has been reactionary.

Ellis finds that war is the worst enemy of civilization. He examines the subject from every side, and can find nothing to say in favour of this, the supreme curse of the human race. He goes rather further than some would be willing to follow him when he thinks that unregulated increase of population is the chief cause of war. That it is one cause is obvious; and indeed the dictatorships deliberately discourage family limitation on the ground that the State needs more food for powder, and that what they call natural expansion of numbers is a justification for the wish of the militant State to dispossess its more pacific or more prudent neighbours of their territory.

Some of our younger eugenists have partly given way to this argument, and agitate for a higher birth-rate at home. Ellis sternly discourages this concession to militarism. He would deliberately prefer a smaller population of higher quality, and he sees that what is called negative eugenics is the only way of preventing a gradual deterioration of our national stock. Nature is more important than nurture, and quality is much more important than quantity.

On almost every question in which science and common sense are ranged against tradition and prejudice, Ellis is found on the right side. He hates and despises the fashionable anti-intellectualism, and is perfectly fearless in following wherever reason leads the way. His influence will take time to soak in, and perhaps the forces of inertia and reaction will be always too strong for his reforms to be adopted; but I know no man in our time who has done more to batter down antiquated prejudice and stupid obscurantism.

He would like to see all doctors Civil Servants, all

hospitals nationalized, and private medical practice abolished. Things seem to be moving in this direction. The Ministry of Health ought, he thinks, to be one of the chief Government offices, with very wide powers. But he is never tired of insisting that those who cry out for "more births" really mean "more deaths," for unregulated increase soon reaches its limits.

There are other sides to his rich and widely sympathetic mind. He was a great traveller, and his favourite countries were France and Spain. He loved to look upon life as an art—even a kind of ritual dance, and he found that the French understand the art of living much better than we do. The life of the average Englishman is not artistic. "Like a sailor on shore, we maintain our equilibrium by rolling heavily from side to side." French civilization has a grace and poise which we cannot emulate.

Not that he disparages his own country and its inhabitants. He loved Cornwall, and East Anglia, the part of England from which his own family came. He was a keen student of architecture, and claims for his countrymen one great invention—the "Perpendicular" church, so well suited to our climate, which needs all the sunlight that we can get. We need not always agree with him. He dislikes the famous west fronts of Wells and Peterborough, and can see nothing to admire in King's Chapel at Cambridge. On the French churches he is an admirable guide.

But the land that he loved best was Spain. In his beautiful book, *The Soul of Spain*, he interprets to us, as none had done before, that strange country of fire and ice, of mysticism and cruelty, of loyalty and anarchism. We should not have expected him to feel any sympathy with the reactionary Catholic Church in the Peninsula; but he loved the Mass as celebrated in Spain, in which he found a solemn dramatic exhibition, "the initiation of the individual into the spiritual life of the world."

And he shuddered to think, as he assisted at these services at Madrid and Barcelona, that before long all this might be swept away in a tornado of bloodshed and destruction. For he knew the dangerous explosives which threatened a violent revolution in Spain, where intolerance on both sides is a tradition.

July, 1939.

VI

PRAISE THE DOCTORS

THE fiftieth anniversary of the foundation of the Pasteur Institute of Paris was celebrated yesterday in the presence of the President of the French Republic and the Minister of Health.

Louis Pasteur was one of the greatest benefactors of humanity, a man of noble character, whose discoveries have revolutionized medical science. Perhaps the time will come when mankind will honour its saviours more than its destroyers, Pasteur and Lister more than Napoleon and Ludendorff.

A year or two ago there was a curious conflict of testimony about the fate of some Russian peasants who had been bitten by a rabid wolf in 1886. They were hurried to Paris to be treated by Pasteur. Dr. Axel Munthe says that they all developed hydrophobia and died raving mad. But Dr. Loir, Pasteur's nephew and assistant, declares that out of twenty-one patients only two died. "The return of the nineteen survivors so impressed the Tsar Alexander III that he sent his cousin, Prince Alexander of Oldenburg, with a present of 300,000 francs to the Pasteur Institute." This seems conclusive; Dr. Munthe must have been misinformed.

There is no body of men whom I respect and

admire so much as the doctors. They are probably better trained for their work than any other profession. They spend their lives in relieving human suffering. They are at the beck and call of their patients day and night; and in my experience they are extraordinarily generous.

The names of the martyrs of medical research ought to be remembered. Rolleston, after a curious list of doctors who have died of their own pet diseases, enumerates fifteen or sixteen victims, some of whom have inoculated themselves experimentally with the disease which they were studying. His list does not include those who have died of blood-poisoning after performing operations, nor the victims of X-ray dermatitis.

I once preached to members of the medical profession in St. Paul's, and after paying them the tribute which I thought due, I suggested that they were rather too reticent in instructing the public about the laws of health, especially perhaps on delicate subjects.

I think this was true when I said it, but there are now a great many popular books. I happen to have in my shelves Rolleston's lectures on *Aspects of Age, Life, and Disease*, Lord Horder's lectures, *Health and a Day*, and Sir Walter Langdon Brown's lectures, *Thus We Are Men*. All these are very interesting. I recommend especially Langdon Brown's lecture on *The Biology of Social Life*.

The doctor has also become a favourite hero in

novels. An amusing collection might be made of medical blunders in fiction. "Brain fever," and "spontaneous combustion" are I believe unknown to science. But some of these novels are by competent doctors.

I have not read *The Citadel*, and do not mean to read it. But I have several medical novels by the writer who calls himself Sidney Fairway, and Brett Young's new book, *Dr. Bradley Remembers*, is a delightful and sympathetic portrait of an undistinguished general practitioner who in his old age could look back on a well-spent life.

These books throw light on the seamy side of the profession. There are dishonest patients who do not pay their bills. There are interlopers who do not observe the etiquette about poaching. There are unlicensed practitioners whom many people trust more than a qualified doctor. It appears that a downright impostor may accumulate a large practice and make money for years, though he is likely to be found out in the end. Sidney Fairway's *A Cuckoo in Harley Street* describes such a career.

The line between a quack and a scientific healer is not always easy to draw. A cynical physician, asked what is the difference between organic and functional disease, answered, "Organic disease is what we try to cure and don't; functional disease is what the quacks say they cure and often do."

The famous Sir William Gull used to maintain

that doctors should practise a little humbug themselves; he did not like it when Dr. Quain or Dr. Martin (the story is told of both) said, "I suppose your patients like to be gulled."

But the new men are all paying attention to psychotherapy. This is what Langdon Brown means by the return to Æsculapius. For Epidaurus, the famous health resort of Greece, was a cunning mixture of Lourdes and Homburg.

I am the fortunate possessor of a little book called *Secret Remedies*, issued in 1909 by the British Medical Association. It analysed and gave the cost price of well-advertised patent medicines. For reasons which may be guessed, this book never found its way to popular circulation. Since then, the composition of every drug has to be stated on the label.

The history of quackery is as old as human nature. Touching for the king's evil (scrofula) went on for centuries, as late as Queen Anne, who touched Samuel Johnson. William III once did it reluctantly, and said to the patient, "God give you better health and more sense."

Sir Kenelm Digby in 1643 advocated "sympathetic powder" for wounds. It was applied to the weapon which caused the wound; the wound was bandaged and let alone. The powder was very successful for this reason.

The great philosopher Berkeley advocated water mixed with tar as a panacea for all diseases.

The homœopathists, of whom I heard much when I was young, were useful in putting a stop to indiscriminate drugging; perhaps that is all that can be said for them. As for bone-setters and osteopaths, it is wiser for a layman to express no opinion.

The co-operation of priest and doctor is a big question. It is not true that most doctors in this country are irreligious men; many of them give admirable spiritual and moral counsel when perplexed or conscience-stricken patients consult them. But the physician of the soul has his own place by the bedside.

It would be well, I think, if some medical teaching could be given at the theological colleges, but not with any idea that the priest should practise as a "healer." That way lies an objectionable kind of quackery.

Some day, it may be hoped, the use of suggestion will be put on a scientific basis. Till this is done, "healers" of all kinds will flourish, for the barbarian in us dearly loves a miracle.

June, 1939.

VII

PROBLEMS OF POPULATION

I HAVE received eight volumes of the Report of the International Congress of Population, held in Paris in 1937. The papers are in four languages, English, French, German and Italian. The whole Report is intensely interesting to me; and I think some points in it will interest those who are not students of vital statistics.

The first is the light which it throws on the race-suicide scare which has filled our newspapers lately, and which has led to a difference of opinion between myself and my old friends of the Eugenics Society.

The maximum population of England and Wales will probably be reached between 1945 and 1950. (My earlier estimate that the high tide would be in 1941 was incorrect.) Accurate prediction is impossible.

How are we to compute the real death-rate? The crude death-rate, as we all know, is quite misleading, and the so-called "standardized" rate, which now has few defenders, is no better. The only satisfactory method is to take the expectation of life at birth, and divide it into 1,000. At present the expectation of life in this country is sixty-one years for both sexes. This divided into 1,000 gives about sixteen and a half. The birth-rate, which seems for the present to have touched bottom three or four years ago, is fifteen. But if the expectation of life were raised to sixty-six or sixty-seven, the figure actually reached in New Zealand, the true death-rate would be fifteen, the same as the birth-rate.

Some of our authorities think that seventy or even seventy-five may be reached, but I think myself that the New Zealand figures are about as good as we are likely to attain. In any case, unless the birth-rate falls still further, though there are no signs of it at present, the scare of depopulation is not justified.

If we were making any effort to people up our Dominions, I should of course be in favour of an increasing population. But we are not. Canada, with three inhabitants to the square mile, and Australia with two, are not likely to remain empty. If we do not develop them, some aggressive nation will step in.

And here Professor Carr-Saunders and Mr. Walshaw give us a serious warning: "The Irish Free State has come to rely upon emigration to prevent over-population." Since the United States will not take them, 80 per cent come to the United Kingdom. Every one of these either comes on the dole or drives an Englishman or Scotsman out of work. "It seems," our authors say, "that the system of helping Englishmen, Welshmen and Scots to leave, while Irish enter, will soon be too illogical to maintain, and that the United Kingdom will have seriously to face the question whether it is going to be peopled from the Irish Free State." Glasgow and Liverpool are asking this question with some bitterness.

If you want to live long, where should you live? In New Zealand by preference. Then come Australia, the Scandinavian countries, Holland, North America and Great Britain.

A well-known writer—I think it was one of the two Huxleys—told us that after fifty the death-rate of American workers is higher than it should be, and that the cause is probably the excessive speeding-up of American labour.

There is a very interesting paper on the length of life under the Roman Empire. The materials are admittedly inadequate, and the results uncertain; but it seems clear that, though North Africa, Spain and Egypt were fairly healthy, the death-rate in Rome was enormous. The average duration of life was only twenty-one years. The figures for the whole Empire, so far as they are procurable, indicate that the average length of life in the most civilized countries has more than doubled in 1,500 years, and nearly all this increase has come within the last two centuries.

The best authorities do not think that the United States will ever hold much more than 200 million people. The fertility of the soil has been recklessly exploited, and there are large tracts where semi-desert conditions prevail. On the other hand, scientific farming is making great strides, and for my own part I think the predicted maximum of 200 million is too low.

There is one other point which I wish to commend especially to any medical men who may do me the honour to read this article. It is well known that, while some diseases are decreasing, others are becoming more deadly. Cancer now kills more people than any other disease except affections of the heart. Dread of this terrible complaint is a nightmare to many people. I suggest that one cause of the apparent increase has not been given sufficient weight.

I have before me an essay on longevity in the United States (in *Population*, February, 1934). Within forty years the mean life of males in Massachusetts has increased from 42·50 years to 59·48 years, of females from 44·46 to 62·74 years. (The figures for our own country are much the same.) But the causes of death have changed in a remarkable way. Of the twenty commonest causes of death in 1900–04 several have disappeared altogether, and new names appear in the list for 1925–9. It is not surprising that automobile accidents, which were infrequent forty years ago, now are No. 10 among the causes of death.

It will be news to many that in spite of the discovery of insulin, the death-rate from diabetes has doubled, and that that from organic heart disease has almost doubled since the beginning of the century.

But the point which I wish to make is this. In the earlier list old age comes ninth on the list; in the later list it does not appear at all. This can only mean one thing—a change in the way of registering deaths. People do not often die of old age pure and simple. The "slight turn of the scale" which, as Sophocles says, "sends to sleep aged bodies," is given by bronchitis or pneumonia or heart failure, and very many old people die not of, but with, cancer.

Forty years ago most of these deaths were certified as due to senile decay; now the proximate cause is given. If all the deaths which were formerly ascribed to senile decay were distributed over the diseases which are common in later life, the increase in some of these, and especially in cancer, would be partially accounted for. It is rash for me, I know, to interfere in a very specialized subject of inquiry, but some eminent physicians do not study statistics, and I have not seen this particular point made.

It is of course a monstrous notion that a nation which makes no effort to keep its numbers within bounds has a moral right to invade its neighbours and dispossess them of their land. But it is not certain that those nations which aim at a very high standard of living have the greatest survival value. Privileged classes as a rule do not keep up their numbers, and privileged nations may have to make way for peoples who are content with fewer comforts.

But one thing seems to have been proved by history. "Peoples that delight in war" do not flourish for long. The most stable civilizations have been those of Asia—India and China, which are not bellicose. Japan has, I think, taken the wrong course, and will pay the penalty.

Quality is more important than quantity, and for this reason I view with some misgiving the policy of choosing out the ablest members of the working class and promoting them into the relatively sterile professional class. It is quite right of course that they should be given their chance, but I am afraid we may be in some danger of skimming off the cream of our population and then throwing it away. Perhaps the differential birth-rate will not always be dysgenic; it is no longer so in Sweden, where, however, the births are too few in all classes.

June, 1939.

LITERATURE

I

DO BOOKS MAKE US WISER?

THOSE who write books are eloquent about the joy of reading. It is natural that they should be. It is their trade, and most of them are great readers themselves. For my own part, I have found more pleasure from books than from anything else. But pleasure is one thing, profit is another. The wise men are not quite so certain that the printed page is the best instructor in the art of living.

I will let the authors speak for themselves, first of the delights of reading, then by way of caution. For a man may form a reading habit, like a drug habit, and it may do him more harm than good.

"Reading makes a full man, talking a ready man, and writing an exact man" (Bacon; but Quintilian said the same thing before him). The "full man," unfortunately, may give himself severe indigestion.

"He that loveth a book will never want a faithful friend, a wholesome counsellor, a cheerful companion, an effectual comforter. By study, by reading, by thinking, one may innocently divert and pleasantly entertain himself, as in all weathers, so in all fortunes" (Barrow).

"Give a man the taste for reading, and the means of gratifying it, and you can hardly fail of making a happy man" (Sir John Herschel).

"I would rather be a poor man in a garret with plenty of books than a king who did not love reading" (Macaulay).

"Libraries are the shrines where all the relics of the ancient saints are preserved and reposed" (Bacon). But may we not plead for a few ancient sinners among them?

"This I am sure of, that I am never long even in the society of her I love without a yearning for the company of my lamp and my utterly confused and tumbled-over library" (Byron). I guess that this confession was made to Mr. Murray, not to the Countess Guiccioli.

"He that hath never fed on the dainties that are bred in a book . . . his intellect is not replenished; he is only an animal, only sensitive in the duller parts" (Shakespeare).

"I have wondered at the patience of the antediluvians; their libraries were insufficiently furnished" (Cowper).

These testimonies—a selection from a large number—are enthusiastic enough; but the cautions are equally emphatic.

"Much learning does not instruct the mind" (Heraclitus). This is repeated by other Greek writers; by Festus to St. Paul, who was not, I think, a great reader; and by Selden: "No man is the wiser for his learning." "To teach children many subjects is dangerous" (Plato). "A crowd of books burdens the learner, and does not instruct him;

it is better to give yourself to a few authors than to ramble among many" (Seneca). *"Non multa sed multum"* is Quintilian's advice.

Great philosophers, says Goethe, have seldom been learned men. The thinkers who are really alive have not belonged to the dreary tribe of commentators. Their philosophy has been their own rule of life; they are men of imagination, poets and prophets. Aristotle is severe on those who, instead of practising a reasoned art of living "take refuge in words and think that they are philosophers."

"Hobbes," says Graham Wallas, "had no patience with those who toil to make broad their bibliographies till they see men as books walking. He was wont to say that if he had read as much as other men he should have known no more than other men."

"He who has experienced nothing is made no wiser by solitude" (Lotze). This must not be taken to mean that George Herbert's advice, "By all means use sometimes to be alone," is wrong, and a student might say that he is not alone when he has a good book to keep him company. We must not despise the life of contemplation; the world owes much to some who have spent most of their lives in lonely communion with God, or with Nature. But Lotze is right in thinking that some experience of mixing with other men is almost essential to wisdom.

Books do not take us quite out of ourselves. We find in them what touches and stimulates our own thoughts. An old rhyme says, "As the fool thinketh, so the bell clinketh." Many people learn more from conversation than from reading. Long talks with like-minded friends are very educating.

In fact, we must recognize that some people are so constituted that they learn by the ear, others by the eye. The former class does not make readers. There are some who would rather listen to a lecture than read a book—an odd taste, I think. But the popularity of broadcasting shows that it is very common.

A half-way house is to listen to a good book read aloud. If the reading is good, nothing can be more delightful. When we read to ourselves, we read too fast and miss some of the best things in the book. Reading aloud takes us along at the right pace, and we have the pleasure of sharing our interest. Poetry should always be read aloud.

It is an interesting question whether, when we take a holiday in some famous beauty spot, as some of us will soon be doing, we want to take with us any of the great poets of Nature, such as Wordsworth, Keats and Shelley. I often pack up my Wordsworth for these holidays, but I must confess that I very seldom read him.

When I am by the sea, which, as Euripides says, "washes away all human ills," or, better still, watch the waves from the deck of a ship; when I stand before a mountain or a waterfall, I do not want to be invited to think of life and death and human folly; I prefer to let Nature speak to me in her own language, which is soothing without being at all explicit.

Dr. Johnson, dragged half against his will to the Highlands, thought it was easier "to sit at home and conceive rocks, heaths and waterfalls." It is, I think, when we recall these scenes in imagination by our firesides, that we are most inclined to enjoy the Nature poets. I dare say I am quite wrong, but such is my own feeling. I read a great deal on a Mediterranean cruise, but not poetry about the sea and the mountains.

We are made very differently, and I pity those who cannot enjoy books. But it is those who enjoy them most who have to beware of intellectual dram-drinking. When we have taken in all that we can digest, it is worse than useless to stuff our minds with good things which we cannot assimilate.

June, 1939.

II

THE POETS IN WAR

PATRIOTISM has always been one of the chief springs of poetry. A victory should be celebrated with songs of triumph, otherwise it may be forgotten. "There were many brave men before Agamemnon," but their memory has perished for want of a Homer. Palestine and Greece were small countries; but the world will never forget the deliverance of Jerusalem from the Assyrians, or the repulse of the Persian invasion.

What a splendid poem is the story of the defeat of the Assyrian host, with its grim finale! "So Sennacherib King of Assyria departed, and went and returned, and dwelt at Nineveh. And it came to pass, as he was worshipping in the house of Nisroch his god, that Adrammelech and Sharezer his sons smote him with the sword: and they escaped into the land of Armenia. And Esarhaddon his son reigned in his stead."

Equally fine is the play of Æschylus about the Battle of Salamis. In both cases a small nation believed that it had been supernaturally delivered from what looked like inevitable subjection by a mighty power. These were grand opportunities for patriotic poetry.

Our poets have on the whole been pacifists. Some
of them, like Thomas Carew in the seventeenth
century, have been isolationists:

> What though the German drum
> Bellow for freedom and revenge, the noise
> Concerns us not, nor should divert our joys,
> Nor ought the thunder of the carabines
> Drown the sweet airs of our tuned violins.

We might make a long list of poets who have
eloquently denounced the wickedness and folly of
war, from John Gower at the end of the fourteenth
century, Thomas Occleve and John Lydgate in the
fifteenth, Thomas Sackville, Earl of Dorset, George
Gascoigne, Humphrey Gifford, Thomas Lodge,
and Edmund Spenser in the sixteenth.

Shakespeare makes his Henry V speak proudly,
even bombastically, on the eve of Agincourt, and
Drayton, in his spirited poem, "Fair stood the wind
for France," boasts in the same strain about the
same battle. The Elizabethans enjoyed full-blooded
rhetoric; but rodomontade of this kind is not really
to our taste.

We are a little ashamed of it. Our soldiers in the
Great War sang grimly humorous songs, quite
unintelligible both to French and Germans, such as:

> Hold down your head, Fusilier;
> There's a b—y great Hun
> With a b—y great gun,
> And he'll blow off your head, Fusilier.

Or:

> Nobody knows how bored we are,
> Bored we are, bored we are,
> Nobody knows how bored we are,
> And nobody seems to care.

The hymn of hate, deadly real to the Germans, was a joke to our men.

At the end of the Civil War England was for a short time the first military power in Europe. "I have seen the English," said Turenne. "They are the finest troops in the world." Our poets under the Protectorate were not pacific. Cromwell's laureate, Marvell, exhorts him to crown his exploits by demolishing our recent allies in the Great War:

> A Cæsar he ere long to Gaul,
> To Italy an Hannibal.

Milton glories in Cromwell's victories, but reminds him that "peace hath her victories not less renowned than war."

In the eighteenth century peace-loving poets are James Thomson, William Collins, Hannah More, and William Cowper.

The long war against Napoleon was the occasion of some of Wordsworth's finest poetry. The picture of the Happy Warrior, "the very perfect gentle knight," was probably meant for Nelson. Not many poems were written about Wellington, and I believe he would have been much annoyed with

Tennyson's famous ode about him. For the Iron Duke, though he was no sentimentalist, hated his own trade. "Anyone," he said, "who has seen even one day of what war really is, would pray God that he may never see another."

Wordsworth's patriotic sonnets came again into their own in the Great War. They are inspired by the conviction that British liberty and British traditions—all that the name of England stands for, are things too precious to be lost. "It is not to be thought of. . . ." These sonnets are worthy of a nation which never lost heart or hope under a prolonged trial.

The last quarter of the nineteenth century saw our country in a bad attack of jingoism which we now wish to forget, but which we ought to remember. It produced some very bad verse of the type of which the "jingo" stanza is a specimen. It would not be fair to class Rudyard Kipling's clean and healthy imperialism with this foolish romanticism of Empire, though Kipling was guilty of stigmatizing foreign nations as "lesser breeds without the law."

Seeley's "Expansion of England" and Froude's "Oceana" appeared just at the right time to add fuel to the flame. Imperialism raged in England till the second jubilee of Queen Victoria. I felt when I watched that procession that this was the culminating point of the British Empire. Two years later came the Boer War, with its humiliations and revelations of incompetence. That was the end of jingoism in this country.

The Great War, which stirred the country to the depths in a way which the Napoleonic War had never done, produced a small quantity of really fine poetry. Some of it may be called the poetry of self-devotion or self-consecration to a cause which was believed to be righteous and holy. Such are the sonnets of Rupert Brooke, and the even more poignant poem of Julian Grenfell. The fact that both of them gave their lives for their country makes it all the more certain that these poems will live as long as the English language is spoken.

Other poems written during the Great War express the patriotism of place, love of home or of some familiar scenes at home. This is a well-defined type of patriotic literature, though not specially connected with war. Sir Walter Scott's "Breathes there the man with soul so dead" expresses the love of a Scot for his native land, which he retains even when, as he so often does, he has wandered far away from it. Wordsworth's love of the Lake District and Matthew Arnold's of the country round Oxford are familiar to all.

Among the poets of the Great War, Rupert Brooke loves to think of his home at Grantchester. Owen, in the little gem beginning "There is a hill in England," looks back with love and gratitude on his days at Harrow; Sorley in the same way remembers Marlborough. Would any Continental soldier remember his schooldays first and foremost when going into action?

There is no boasting, no swagger, no hatred of the enemy in any of these poems. But the poetry of the Great War has one feature which is perhaps new. Several of the men who went through that awful experience write with concentrated bitterness, not against the enemy, but against the civilians who made the War and sent millions of young men to the shambles without any real necessity. The poems of Siegfried Sassoon are unlike any war poetry written before. Even if his accusations are not always just, they are a terrible indictment, and, as we have seen, the victor of Waterloo would perhaps not have disapproved.

So far as I can see, the evil spirits of aggression, of vainglory, of hatred and contempt of other nations have been exorcized, we may hope finally, from this country. As for Machiavelli and his doctrine that the State can do no wrong, a doctrine now openly avowed and acted on by some of our neighbours, most of us would agree with John Wesley, who wrote:

"My cool judgment is that if all the other doctrines of devils which have been committed to writing since letters were in the world were collected together in one volume, it would fall short of this; and that should a Prince form himself by this book, so calmly recommending hypocrisy, treachery, lying, robbery, oppression and murder, Domitian or Nero would be an angel of light compared to that man."

And yet—we cannot cast out devils by Beelzebub, the chief of the devils.

August, 1939.

III

DID SHAKESPEARE UNLOCK HIS HEART?

"WHEN a man is unhappy," said Coleridge to Southey, "he writes infernally bad poetry." If I were very unhappy, I should be even less inclined to write poetry than at other times. Seneca, in one of the best lines of his tragedies, which nobody reads now, says, "Small troubles talk; great troubles are dumb" (*Curæ leves loquuntur, ingentes stupent*).

This may seem to contradict the words of Shelley:

> Most wretched men
> Are cradled into poetry by wrong;
> They learn in suffering what they teach in song.

But are the poets miserable when they are making their rhymes? I doubt it.

Some writers I admit, groan and curse sincerely enough both in verse and prose. Some are mad; some are stung with remorse; some shed tears of self-pity; some are troubled by their livers. Some have been crossed in love; but this, as Shakespeare says, is never fatal. I think Coleridge is right that unhappiness seldom produces great poetry.

Was Tennyson overcome with grief when he wrote *In Memoriam*? Hallam's death caused him great distress, but I think he had recovered from it.

275

He seems to me to have been more worried by the problems of his semi-Christianity than by his bereavement.

No great poet has suffered more than Shakespeare from the false notion that a poet must have lived through all the experiences which he describes. Shakespeare was a dramatist; it was his business to represent human nature, not his own, in many different aspects.

"The truest poetry is the most feigning," he says himself. But because we know comparatively little about his life, industrious and romantic commentators must make up imaginary biographies of the man, telling us how he wrote tragedies when he was unhappy and comedies when he was merry, and how his life was almost wrecked by a mysterious dark lady.

I believe that all this is pure imagination. Wordsworth thought that Shakespeare, once at least, "unlocked his heart." If he did, Robert Browning retorted, "the less Shakespeare he." George Meredith fancied Shakespeare shouting with laughter over his commentators.

My own impression of Shakespeare is that he was a supremely normal man. His contemporaries describe him as "gentle"; he was good company and enjoyed society—what the Americans call a good mixer. He relished the good things of life and lived in the best house in his native town.

Why he gave up writing at the age of forty-seven,

when he was at the height of his powers and reputation, we shall never know. Has anyone suggested that the last five years of his life were spent in writing the works of Bacon?

He was not at all the kind of man to be pulled off his balance by any dark lady. His convictions about love and marriage were both sane and high-minded. The noble sonnet, "Let me not to the marriage of true minds . . ." is unquestionably sincere, as are the lines in *Venus and Adonis*:

> Love's gentle spring doth always fresh remain;
> Lust's winter comes ere summer half be done.

Our modern critics, it is needless to say, are angry with Shakespeare for writing *Measure for Measure*, and wonder whether he really admired Isabella, "wrapt in her selfish chastity." Shakespeare certainly admired her, and knew that those who heard the play would admire her, too. Our new critics call Isabella a type of true puritanism. She is meant to be a type not of puritanism but of purity.

But the sonnets? They are not dramatic; did not Shakespeare unlock his heart here? No, he did not; he was writing fashionable verse, which produces an illusion of intense feeling, because the author was already a great writer. In France and Italy sonnets addressed to great persons were common in the sixteenth century; in England the fashion was followed by Wyatt, Surrey and Sidney.

Then came long sonnet sequences on the pleasures and pains of love, after the manner of Petrarch. Almost all aspirants to poetry tried their hands at this kind of composition. Shakespeare wrote many of his sonnets when he was twenty-nine or thirty; but he was not above copying the queer conceit of writing as an elderly man. This curious trick is proved by C. J. Sisson in a lecture to which this *causerie* is much indebted.

Daniel was twenty-nine when he wrote, "My years draw on my everlasting night, My days are done"; Bamfield was only twenty when he wrote, "Behold my grey head full of silver hairs." When Shakespeare in his plays refers to sonnet-writing, the reference, I think, is always contemptuous.

Other commonplaces of this kind of composition, with no genuine experience behind them, were remonstrances against a young man's "unthrifty loveliness," vituperations of a cruel siren, and anticipations of immortality for his verses, which were common form in sonnets, copied from Horace, Ovid and other old writers.

Shakespeare's sonnets are among the glories of English poetry. But the framework is thoroughly conventional, and it is useless to look in them for materials for a biography of the poet.

This view of Shakespeare will not be accepted by most people. For example, Mr. Middleton Murry, who does justice to the noble but thoroughly human and natural pictures of love in the plays, thinks that

278

"no one but a briefed advocate could assert that the sonnets do not contain the record of the poet's own disaster in love."

I do not agree. Very few men could describe the woes of disappointed love so well without having experienced them. But Shakespeare was one of the few; and he had excellent models in this very popular kind of composition.

I am not so confident that Mr. Murry is wrong when he finds bitter cynicism in *Measure for Measure*, *Troilus and Cressida* and *All's Well That Ends Well*. But I am not convinced.

I fear we must be on our guard against accepting any writer's literary pose as a revelation of his real character. Matthew Arnold, the apostle of sweetness and light, was a great, broad-shouldered, genial Englishman; the soft-hearted Dickens and the idealist Carlyle left fortunes; Thomas Hardy, the pessimist, was a cheerful person in private life. Perhaps a poet may throw himself into a mood of woe; but we are never so happy or so unhappy as we think ourselves—poets perhaps least of all.

September, 1938.

IV

THE PILGRIM'S PROGRESS

On the thirty-first of August, 1688, died the greatest of all allegorists, the author of one of the great religious books of the world, one of the glories of our race and literature, the tinker, John Bunyan.

The Pilgrim's Progress is said to exist in 124 different languages, a number which must, I should think, nearly exhaust a complete list of the varieties of human speech. It is part of the education of children of every religion. Children love Bunyan, for he is a prince of story-tellers. They never forget Giant Despair and his grievous crabtree cudgel, nor the trial of Faithful before Mr. Justice Hategood.

Even Roman Catholic children are allowed to read an expurgated copy, from which Giant Pope has disappeared.

He was born at Elstow, near Bedford, in 1628. He is commonly called a Baptist; but as he had two of his children baptized in infancy, it is better to call him unsectarian. He lived as a poor man among the poor, and owes very little to other writers, except the English Bible, that well of pure English undefiled.

Like his contemporary George Fox, he spent many years of his life in prison. Prison in those days might mean anything from a noisome dungeon to a mild detention like St. Paul's two years' captivity at Rome. Bunyan was allowed to read and write and see his friends. He preached in the gaol, and occasionally outside it.

In his later years—he died at sixty—he was very famous. No fewer than 100,000 copies of *The Pilgrim's Progress* were sold during his lifetime.

In the most beautiful war memorial in England, the cloister or Campo Santo at Winchester College, the scholars who helped the architect to plan it searched for the best motto they could find in all literature. They found it in the writings of the humble tinker of Bedford, who knew no language but his own, yet brought a new music out of the English tongue. It is from the description of how Mr. Valiant-for-Truth crossed the river at the end of his pilgrimage:

"My sword I give to him that shall succeed me in my pilgrimage, and my courage and skill to him that can get it. My marks and scars I carry with me, to be a witness for me that I have fought his battles, who now will be my rewarder. So he passed over, and all the trumpets sounded for him on the other side."

The last sentence was chosen for the memorial to the choristers of St. Paul's Cathedral who gave their lives for their country in the Great War.

In reading Bunyan, we need not trouble ourselves whether his doctrine is always orthodox. Christianity has never been divided in the region where he lived and prayed and wrote. His theology rests on his intense conviction—his "smarting" conviction, to use his own word—of the tremendous reality of the choice between right and wrong.

He was a soldier in his youth, though, oddly enough, it is not quite certain whether he fought for the King or the Parliament (probably the latter), and he thought of the Christian life not only as a pilgrimage, but as a campaign, as he shows in his later book, *The Holy War*.

Bunyan's was the strength of Sir Galahad; for though he reproaches himself bitterly for cursing and swearing before his conversion, he testifies, against certain calumniators, that never in his life had he transgressed the Christian law of purity. He thanks God that no woman has been the worse for him.

The theme of the allegory is based on a fine passage in the Epistle to the Hebrews. "They confessed that they were strangers and pilgrims on the earth. For they that say such things declare plainly that they seek a country. And truly if they had been mindful of that country from which they came out, they might have had the opportunity to return. But now they desire a better country, that is a heavenly."

There never was a time when men more needed to remember that "our citizenship is in heaven," for our religion has been secularized far too much. For we are dealing with spiritual things, in which the language of time and place, however necessary it may be as a help to our imaginations, is misleading.

We are not literally travelling through an alien country to another place where God dwells. We are not literally turning our backs on the City of Destruction. Heaven and hell are within us; for heaven is wherever the Spirit of God deigns to dwell, and hell is wherever He has been shut out, and evil spirits have been suffered to enter in.

Nor does the world through which we are hurrying, in fear of being waylaid or falling into pitfalls or taking a wrong turn which may be a way to perdition, mean exactly human society.

We are bidden not to love the world nor the things that are in the world. But these are explained as the lust of the flesh, the lust of the eyes, and the pride of life. "The world passeth away and the lust thereof, but he that doeth the will of God abideth for ever." But there is much in human society which belongs to the pure, the holy, the indestructible.

I am fond of a sentence in Plotinus: "Even wickedness is human, being mixed with something contrary to itself." The muddiest parts of the road are where we are floundering in the mess that we have made ourselves. Neither in time nor in place must we separate the present life too absolutely from that which is to come. This world is that part of God's creation in which our lot is cast.

The great moralists always see life in silhouette.

Evil and good for them are black and white. It is this tremendous moral earnestness, this haunting conviction of the infinite importance of the choice, which makes Bunyan's allegory a very great book.

And in these days when over half the Continent men will swear that black is white to save their skins, it is refreshing to read what Bunyan wrote from prison.

"If nothing will do unless I make of my conscience a continual butchery and slaughter-shop, unless putting out my own eyes I commit me to the blind to lead me, I have determined, the Almighty God being my help and shield, yet to suffer, if frail life might continue so long, even till the moss shall gow on my eyebrows rather than thus to violate my faith and principles."

> He's a slave that would not be
> In the right with two or three.

So Lowell wrote, and so Bunyan lived.

August, 1938.

V

AUTOBIOGRAPHIES

ROBERT BURNS, in two very familiar lines, wishes for that "giftie" which would give us the power of seeing ourselves as others see us.

For my own part, when I lie awake thinking of all the idiotic things I have done in seventy-eight years, I console myself with the reflection that since no living person knows more than a small fraction of these idiocies, it is impossible that others can see me as I see myself. And yet people write autobiographies !

Sir Leslie Stephen suggested that everyone should write his own life, and leave it sealed up with his will. No self-portrait, he thinks, can be dull, for the topic is one in which we are keenly interested, and on which we are the highest living authority.

But does the autobiographer wish to tell the truth about himself, and does he know the truth about himself? That, Stephen says, does not matter. The book may be more valuable in proportion to the amount of misrepresentation which it contains.

Men so often give false characters to their neighbours that we may be curious to see how a man fares when he writes a false testimonial to himself. The dullest of us may succeed in explaining how we came to be so very dull.

The autobiographer, we may guess, usually has a good conceit of himself. His life is an interesting novel, of which he is the hero. Some men, I think, make up their minds early in life what they mean to do and to be, and act that part as if they had already achieved their ambition. Then they write their own lives in canonicals or gold lace or ermine or frock coats, according to the figure which they desire to make in the world.

But sometimes they have a naïve wish to take the public into their confidence. They do not mind confessing their foibles, which do not prevent them from loving and admiring themselves.

Some people must find a peculiar pleasure in making confessions, or "sharing," as the Groupists say. "I am sometimes troubled," said Boswell to Johnson, "by a disposition to stinginess." "So am I," was Johnson's reply, "but I do not tell it." Few of us would willingly own to this weakness.

Rousseau I suppose was mad. The account he gives of himself in his autobiography is most repulsive, and yet he is calmly convinced that as compared with others he is a very virtuous man.

Benvenuto Cellini was a typical Italian of the Renaissance, an artist to the finger-tips, without any moral sense whatever. He tells us with equal gusto of the perfect proportions of his statue of Perseus, and how neatly he planted a dagger in the nape of his enemy's neck.

What are we to say of Samuel Pepys? When we

read his pious resolutions on Sunday, we fully expect to find three asterisks in his entry for Thursday. How can any man have wished to leave a record of such humiliating weakness?

Well, Pepys was a young man; he lived in the reign of Charles II, and he wrote in a shorthand which he probably did not intend to be deciphered. I think he wrote with a view to his own delectation in his old age, when, as La Rochefoucauld says, men console themselves by giving good advice for being no longer able to give a bad example. In any case, we readily forgive Pepys, and are grateful to him for one of the most amusing books ever written.

Of a very different type are the confessions of high-minded and religious men. These include some of the great books of the world. I have written before about Marcus Aurelius. He was a Stoic saint, and Stoicism, though a creed for heroes, makes a man hard and unsympathetic. The Christian form of Stoicism is Calvinism.

St. Augustine's *Confessions* are an intensely interesting self-portrait. They were written many years after his conversion to Christianity; and when we compare them with several short treatises, which hardly anyone reads, written at the time when he was making up his mind to become a Christian, we cannot help being afraid that his memory has not been altogether accurate. Still, the *Confessions* are a very great book, and the revelation of a very noble character.

A modern book of the same class is the *Journal Intime* of Professor Amiel of Geneva. The interest of this record of an uneventful life is partly in the brilliant philosophical, religious and literary criticisms of which it is full, and partly in the rather wearisome self-tormenting which he relieved his mind by describing at length in his diary.

On this it is only necessary to say that the prudishness of his first editors withheld the true psychological explanation, which is now evident enough. "It is not good for man to be alone." But his friends do not seem to have found him melancholy.

George Fox and John Bunyan would have us believe that they were great sinners before their conversion. There was probably not much to be ashamed of, but saints judge themselves very severely.

Many of us have been reading Mr. Low's excellent life of the historian Gibbon. His autobiography does not reveal a very noble character; at times he seems to have made himself ridiculous. But he is the supreme example of a man who knew exactly what he could do, and did it. He actually finished his immortal history.

We smile at the man who "sighed as a lover, but obeyed as a son," and suspect that the sighs were not very afflicting. But many others have done the same, without expressing themselves so epigrammatically.

Herbert Spencer's enormous autobiography has

done his reputation no good. He proved that a prophet may be totally devoid of the sense of humour, and this has helped to degrade him from a major to a minor prophet. Mill's autobiography is much more interesting.

Books of reminiscences are not autobiography. They may be very interesting when the author has lived among distinguished people and shared in interesting events. Books like the *Greville Memoirs* and *Creevey's Diary* belong to social and political history.

But writers of reminiscences are bound in honour to be more discreet than they always show themselves. Table-talk ought not to be repeated, though the temptation to do so may be severe. And if we have any reason to fear that somebody may write a memoir of ourselves, we should be careful about keeping private letters from celebrities.

> Lives of great men oft remind us,
> When we o'er their pages turn,
> That we too may leave behind us
> Letters that we ought to burn.

Whether it was right to burn Byron's diary we shall never know. It probably contained some rather lurid confessions, but nothing worse than what he was suspected of.

VI

CRIME STORIES

MANY years ago I was sitting next at dinner to Sir Basil Thomson, the head of Scotland Yard. I asked him which detective novel he thought the best. He said, *Trent's Last Case*.

"What do you think of Sherlock Holmes?"

"Some of his plots are very good, and are even interesting to us from the professional point of view. But of course we really rely on information, not on deduction. Otherwise we should have run in an archbishop before now."

I remembered that he was the son of an archbishop. His remark suggested a delightful incident, in which his Grace of York was arrested on a charge of murder by his son, and only released, when the case looked black against him, by the superhuman acumen of Sherlock Holmes or Monsieur Poirot or Mr. Fortune.

Detective novels usually represent the official detectives as self-confident and rather stupid. I have only once had dealings with Scotland Yard.

During the War I received a letter from France, purporting to come from a lady who had once been in our employment. She wished me to sign a document which would enable her to return to England.

On seeing the letter, my wife said at once, "This is not Miss ——'s handwriting." So we sent the letter, with an old letter undoubtedly written by the lady, to the Yard, and I said that it looked like an attempt at impersonation, perhaps by a spy. The authorities ought to have consulted an expert on handwriting, who would probably have told them, as proved to be the case, that the second letter was genuine, but in a disguised handwriting. Instead of this, they took a great deal of trouble in hunting up the antecedents of the lady, against whom there was no suspicion whatever.

The spy mania gave Scotland Yard a great deal of trouble. Our organist at St. Paul's reported that while fishing in Sutherland he had observed two very suspicious-looking individuals prowling about. He was told that the Yard had just received similar information from the same place. My friend had been stalking two harmless tourists, and they had been stalking him.

The novelist's amateur sleuth-hound generally has some characteristics in common. He is very much addicted to tippling between meals. He gives extravagant tips on all occasions. He is a connoisseur of good wine and good food. He has certain tricks of phrase by which we recognize him.

The plots are apt to be rather too complicated. We are introduced to several people who might have committed the crime, and the experienced reader guesses that the real culprit will not be the person who is at first suspected. Sometimes we are not convinced that the villain, whose villainy has been too carefully disguised, could have done the deed.

In the earlier novels, such as those of Conan Doyle, half the stories had nothing to do with murder. But the public, it seems, now cares for nothing except murder. This is a curious feature of popular taste. There is great excitement when a dead body is found, and there is a hue and cry after the murderer quite different in intensity to what is roused by an undetected burglary or arson.

In real life, what proportion of poisoners are convicted? I once asked the question of a well-known medical expert, and if I understood him rightly he thought that the majority of poisoners are unsuspected, or at least unconvicted.

One celebrated doctor left it on record that he knew of a poison which could not be detected. He resolved that the secret should die with him.

Our country comes out almost best in statistics of homicide. We are a humane people, indisposed to crimes of violence. Murder is most frequent in lands where lethal weapons are carried, and where criminals usually escape punishment. Americans are very properly ashamed of the bad record of their country in this respect.

Why are detective novels so popular? It is a craze, like crossword puzzles, but it has had a long run. I suppose peaceable citizens like to escape in imagination to a world in which the Ten Commandments, or at least one or two of them, do not run. (A waggish examinee, asked what he thought of the Decalogue as a code of morals, wrote, "Candidates should attempt number seven, and at last four others !") There is also the pleasure of guessing, of solving a problem.

We cannot afford to be disdainful of this attraction. I know several highly intellectual men who revel in detective stories. Personally, I am getting rather tired of them, but I have read a great many. They make excellent reading for a railway journey, when one does not feel inclined for very severe mental exertion.

I have quoted an expert professional opinion as to which is, or was twenty years ago, the best crime-novel. I do not know whether Gaboriau's novels, which may perhaps be said to have founded this type, are as good as or better than those of Conan Doyle and his followers. But of one thing I am sure. A good crime-novel ought to have other topics of interest besides the problem how to find the guilty person.

It ought, in fact, to be a real novel as well as a puzzle. Conan Doyle's longer crime-stories are not his best, but there have been some recent books which fulfil this condition.

The best of all, in my opinion, is one of the earliest—Wilkie Collins's masterpiece, *The Moonstone*. The theft of the sacred jewel from the Indian temple, and the devoted quest of the three Indians to recover it and to punish the robbers, make the book interesting from first to last, and the dénouement is quite unexpected enough, though not unnatural.

His other once-famous novels, *The Woman in White* and *No Name*, are well worth reading, but in my opinion not equal to *The Moonstone*.

What will be the next experiment of the harassed novelist, who has to provide something new when almost all "avenues" have been "explored"? Psychology may be inexhaustible; but a profound study of character requires very unusual ability. The sex novel, so popular on the Continent, is very wearisome, and the study of social types, as in Arnold Bennett's novels, makes one doubt sometimes whether all social types are worth minute study.

However, if this work is well done, it may acquire a historical interest. The revival of Anthony Trollope is very significant. Middle-class life under Queen Victoria lives again in the Barchester novels. Jane Austen has immortalized herself by showing what people did and thought about during the Napoleonic war. Apparently they never thought about their country, which was then fighting for its existence and for the liberties of Europe.

Some are beginning to read Miss Yonge for a truthful picture of one corner of English life two or three generations ago. My parents brought us up on her novels, parts of which make queer reading now.

The giants, Scott, Dickens and Thackeray, belong to all time. If our young people do not read them, we can only be very sorry for them.

February, 1939.

VII

H. G. WELLS AS PESSIMIST

WE shall all be reading *The Fate of Homo Sapiens*. Even those of us who like our Wells better as a novelist than as a prophet cannot help reading all that he writes. He is absolutely honest and in deadly earnest.

But I must confess that I am disappointed with this last book of his. Perhaps at seventy we do not get rid of our prejudices; I know I have not got rid of mine. Wells still has an animus against the "upper classes." (Our inverted snobbery has reached such a pitch that we shall soon begin to give our addresses apologetically as "Upper" Tooting or "High" Wycombe.) He speaks of democracy and socialism as if they were the same thing, though the world is moving towards bureaucratic State capitalism.

Above all, he does not see that most people are deeply attached to values which mean little to him, such as allegiance to God, King and Country. We must take human nature as it is, and these loyalties will continue to determine the actions of human beings. We should be much happier if we were all good Europeans; but we do not seem to be moving in that direction. Nations hate each other with a poisonous and irrational hatred.

Wells thinks that *homo sapiens* is in imminent danger of co-operative suicide because we have changed our environment much too rapidly to adapt ourselves to new conditions. We may perish like the dinosaurs, which could not adapt themselves to changes of climate. I am not sure that I agree.

No doubt the advances in technology have created serious new problems. But I do not think the changes in the present century have been so great as those at the time of the Renaissance, when almost at the same time printing put the Bible and other books in the hands of all; when Columbus and Vasco da Gama revealed a new world beyond the seas, and Copernicus and Galileo a new world beyond the skies; when gunpowder revolutionized warfare, and Europe awoke from the night of the Dark Ages with the Greek and Latin classics in her hands.

It is an interesting theory that war was once a biological necessity, a blood-letting to prevent over-population. Modern war bears no resemblance to even old-fashioned surgery. It is an unmitigated evil. And yet, Wells thinks, many of our troubles are due to the presence of unemployed young men, idle hands for whom Satan finds mischief to do. The social stability of the last century was largely due to emigration. Now there are no more lands open to emigration.

The tone of the book is one of extreme pessimism.

"War is a galloping consumption of the human species." Our country is "fatuously content with itself and unaware of its continual decadence."

Is there really any justification for this despairing attitude? We are masters of our environment as we have never been before. It is admitted that the world can feed and clothe itself without difficulty. The average duration of life has been doubled, and we are learning how to regulate our numbers without the old expedients of war and infanticide. In the most advanced countries civilization has reached nearly the whole population, instead of only one class.

The author would apparently like to abolish private property and national boundaries, and he is disappointed that he is not likely to see either of these reforms brought about. But he also thinks that we are on the brink of a catastrophe which will finally ruin civilization. The villain who may accomplish this is of course Hitler, whom he believes to be insane.

Has Mr. Wells been to Germany lately? Where did he encounter these bloodthirsty criminals? There are some German jingoes of course who want to paint Europe their particular colour. There is not the slightest reason to think that they desire war with either France or England.

If we are foolish enough to go to war about Danzig, what then? Is all over with civilization, as Wells assumes? No one has more reason to view the

298

prospect of war with horror than I have. I have three sons of military age. Another war would destroy almost everything that I care about. It would complete the ruin of the class to which I have the misfortune to belong. It would bring to an end the pleasant, simple, hospitable country-house life which is the fine flower of our civilization. It would give the *coup de grâce* to our public schools, which are already in difficulties. The England which would emerge from a great war would be a country in which I should be sorry to have to live.

But when our prophets go further, and say that another war would be the end of civilization, are they not exaggerating? To begin with, the ruin would overtake only part of Europe, the smallest of the continents. The New World would survive intact, and would preserve our traditions and discoveries, which therefore would not be lost.

It is generally supposed that if there is another war, one side or the other will be knocked out in much less than four years. There are not the same vast reserves of capital that existed in 1914. The losses would therefore in all probability be smaller than in the Great War. In the Great War it is estimated that 10 million men were killed in action, and that nearly 15 million died in the great epidemic of influenza in 1918. The loss of wealth was incalculable. And yet in 1928 there were more people in the world and more wealth in the world than in 1914. Both population and wealth rapidly find their own level, like water. There will always be as many Englishmen in England as there is room for, unless we do what we are doing now, and admit the most undesirable of immigrants (I do not mean the refugees) by thousands into Great Britain every year.

The air menace has, I think, been exaggerated. Madrid and Barcelona were bombed day after day for months. Much damage was done, but photographs show that the general aspect of the streets is much as it was; at any rate those cities are not in ruins.

In fact, I think Wells wrote this book in a bad fit of the blues. This is not a cheerful time to live in, and our foolish promises in Eastern Europe, which we could not fulfil without the help of Russia, who I think has an understanding with Hitler, may land us in sad trouble. But war, though more destructive, is less frequent than formerly. In the century before Waterloo we were more often at war than in peace. And I do not think our people are decadent, though our home base is too small for us to remain a great world Power.

August, 1939.

MISCELLANEOUS

I

HOW MUCH DO YOU OWE TO LUCK?

NEAR the end of the new *Life of Lord Haldane* by Sir Frederick Maurice there is a passage which interested me very much. It is quoted from Lord Haldane's autobiography, and was written only a short time before his death:

"I would not, if I could, take the chance of living life over again. A distinguished living statesman and man of the world once asked me whether, even with the aid of such knowledge as experience had brought, I would like to try to begin life anew. My answer was in the negative. For, he added, we are apt greatly to underrate the part which accident and good luck have really played in the shaping of our careers and in giving us such successes as we have had. I would not myself try again, for I do not feel sure that good fortune, irrational as it has been, would attend me in the same way."

There are not many successful men who have owed less to luck than Haldane, unless we call it luck to have been born with a brain which made him a brilliantly successful lawyer, "the best War Minister England has ever had" (this was Lord Haig's considered opinion), and one of the leading philosophers of his time. But even he, as well as his distinguished friend (was it Asquith?) thought that chance had played so great a part in his career that he would not care to hazard another experiment.

Can anyone, in looking back on his life, deny that it has been a chapter of accidents? Have we been moderately successful? Well, our parents chose a good school, and very nearly chose a bad one.

Our valuable lives have several times just escaped being cut short. I myself have twice missed by a few inches having my brains knocked out, once by a cricket-ball and once by a bullet which whizzed through a railway carriage in which I was sitting.

If we have had the supreme happiness of a perfect marriage, was it not chance that brought us together? And how narrowly, perhaps, we escaped a less enviable fate! We have gained appointments? Yes, we happened to be under the tree when the apple fell.

The religious mind may talk of chance being "overruled." As Pope says with his shallow optimism, "All nature is but art unknown to thee; all chance direction which thou canst not see." It may be so, but it does not look like it. Sir William Harcourt said: "Some men deserve honours and do not get them, and others get them who do not deserve them; so on the whole justice is done." A satisfactory kind of justice to those who get the honours, but not to the others.

I can see very few signs of justice in the world,

and I dare not assert more than St. Paul says: "What hast thou that thou didst not receive? But if thou didst receive it, why dost thou glory as if thou hadst not received it?" And who are we to despise those who have failed, as we might so easily have failed ourselves?

Some writers, like Lytton Strachey and H. G. Wells, seem to have a positive resentment against those whom history calls great, and to take a mischievous pleasure in dragging them off their pedestals. Were Julius Cæsar and Napoleon supermen after all? If they had lived a little earlier or later, or in some other part of the world, would they have done much?

They knew it themselves, when they talked about their star or their fortune. "I could not replace myself," Napoleon said. Perhaps it is true that the world knows nothing of its greatest men. In any case, it is time that we left off making heroes of successful brigands who did not scruple "to wade through slaughter to a throne, and shut the gates of mercy on mankind." Better to be a mute, inglorious Milton, born at the wrong time and place and so condemned to obscurity.

It is a fascinating speculation, what part pure chance has played on a grand scale in history. We might find a dozen instances when the history of civilization for centuries has depended on mere accident. I will choose two, the immense importance of which cannot be disputed.

Alexander the Great, as we all know, conquered Asia as far as the Indus in a few years, and died at the age of thirty-two of a fever which he caught at Babylon. He was imprudent in drinking heavily and taking a cold bath with a high temperature, but his early death was, we may say, a matter of chance.

We need not discuss whether he was really a great man; perhaps his father Philip was abler than he was; but he had boundless ambitions, and his army was invincible. Hannibal never took a fortified town; but Alexander captured three of the strongest fortresses of antiquity, Thebes, Gaza and Tyre.

If he had lived, he would have certainly turned his attention to the west, where Greek colonies were threatened by Carthage and Rome. Livy thought that the Romans would have beaten him, but they would not, especially as some of the warlike Italian tribes would have helped him. They at least would have voted for wiping Rome off the map. Can we imagine the course of history with no Roman Empire, no Latin languages and no Roman Church? That microbe at Babylon may have altered the course of events for thousands of years.

There was another conqueror who equalled the success of Alexander in the reverse direction—Renan's "ugly little Jew," Saul of Tarsus. After his conversion, the Jews of Damascus tried to murder him, and he only escaped by being "let down from the wall in a basket." If his enemies had succeeded in killing him, would Christianity have petered out as an obscure Jewish heresy, which survived for two or three generations as a kind of Khalifate in the family of the Founder?

The religion of Christ, as the event proved, had no future among the Semites; it is the least Asiatic of the great religions. Without St. Paul, would it ever have attacked and at last conquered Græco-Roman civilization? If not, what would be our religion to-day?

These are questions which can never be answered. But those philosophers who hold that "the real is the rational," and that history is the inevitable working-out of "the idea," seem to me to ignore the obvious fact that in great things and small, in the lives of nations and of individuals, things might have turned out very differently. Those only who put their trust in the eternal and unchanging verities can smile at Fortune, a goddess with many votaries.

Others, if in their old age, they have attained some of their ambitions, may, like Lord Brougham in his villa at Cannes, take as their motto the epigram which exists in various forms in Greek, Latin and English:

> I've entered port. Fortune and Hope, adieu;
> Make game of others, for I've done with you.

June, 1939.

307

II

SEVENTY-NINE YEARS OLD

"Though men be so strong that they come to four-score years, yet is their strength then but labour and sorrow."

Well, I entered upon my eightieth year on the sixth of June and I do not quite agree with the Psalmist. It is true that I shirked the 2,000 feet climb to the citadel of Corinth, though I knew I was missing one of the grandest views in the world; but I did not want to go, and remained contentedly on the flat. My life is not all labour and sorrow.

Still, I do not think a wise man would wish for a very long life. "Superfluous lags a veteran on the stage," says Samuel Johnson, who also confesses that "the return of my birthday, if I remember it, fills me with thoughts which it seems to be the general care of humanity to escape." That great and good man was curiously afraid of death.

If we have retired from our business, we cannot flatter ourselves that we are of much more use in the world. If we have resolved to "die in harness"— in other words to stick to our emoluments till "six braw gentlemen kirkward shall carry us," we ought to know, if we do not, that we are obstructing the traffic.

It is not easy to move with the times. The young

have their own ideas, which are not ours. "The conversation of the young and old," says Dr. Johnson again, "generally ends with contempt or pity on either side." Young men have long ago begun to call us "Sir." At last comes the final humiliation, when a pretty girl offers us her seat in an omnibus.

Most of our friends are gone. The causes which we believed in are discredited or out of fashion. "It is enough to drive us old folk mad," wrote Goethe in 1811, "when we see the world round us falling into decay, slipping back into chaos until, God knows when, a new cosmos will arise."

If an old man has given hostages to fortune, there are very few possibilities that can give him any pleasure, and many that he can hardly bear to think of—disasters to his country, and the strokes of Fate falling, not on himself, that matters hardly at all, but on his family and friends.

There are, no doubt, compensations. To be free from the spur of ambition, and from the sting of unruly appetites, makes old age peaceful. Swift thought that "no wise man ever wished to be younger," which is not true; Swift was a morbid melancholiac; but I do not think any wise man would choose to be artificially rejuvenated by Voronoff.

The Greeks had a proverb: "The deeds of the young, the counsels of the middle-aged, the prayers of the old." But prayer, rightly understood, is the communion of the soul with eternal truth.

Mimnermus, the Greek love-poet, wished to die at sixty because "life is nothing without golden Aphrodite." Napoleon declared that "after sixty a man is worth nothing." He himself was worth very little after forty-seven; so, it appears, was Shakespeare; they both died at fifty-two. But I much prefer Sir Thomas Overbury's "a good man feels old age more by the strength of his soul than by the weakness of his body"; or St. Paul's "though our outward man perish, yet our inward man is renewed day by day."

The old live much in memories of the past. Much of our past is lost to us; but here and there peaks rise mysteriously clear out of the mist. Are we better or worse than we were forty or fifty years ago? "Every man over forty is a scoundrel," says Bernard Shaw. "I hope," said Benjamin Jowett, "that our young men will not grow into such dodgers as these old men are." "An old man," said Halifax, "concludeth from his knowing mankind that they know him too, and that maketh him very wary."

I am afraid it is true that a kind of sclerosis of the conscience often sets in at about fifty. We have come to take ourselves as well as our wives for better and for worse. We have come to terms with our characters, despairing of being able to mend them. We will serve God and Mammon in moderation. We have not renounced the world, the flesh and the devil, but they must not get us into scrapes. I fear this state of mind is too common; but how many shining exceptions there are !

"In the decline of life," to quote Johnson once more, "shame and grief are of short duration." Keyserling thinks that we may decline responsibility for things we did more than fifteen years ago. It is a consoling thought; but if we can remember any ingratitude, want of affection or sympathy, or crass selfishness towards those who once loved us and whom we have lost, the wound smarts for much more than fifteen years.

The old man looks forward as well as back. What do we really feel about survival and immortality? Tennyson said that if he did not believe in personal survival he would put his face in a chloroformed handkerchief and have done with it all. Browning believed in reincarnation:

> I shall thereupon
> Take rest, ere I begone
> Once more on my adventure brave and new.

For myself, I feel more and more that the conscious *ego* is not the real self. I am frankly tired of the "body of our humiliation," and have no wish to see it resuscitated. Nor do I look forward to any future in time and place—certainly not to the kind of survival which our misguided necromancers dream of. In the world of spirits "there shall be time no longer." Goethe writes to Eckermann: "When a man is seventy-five he cannot help sometimes thinking about death. The thought of it leaves me perfectly calm, for I am convinced that our spirit is absolutely indestructible. It is something that works on from eternity to eternity; it is like the sun which only seems to sink and in reality never sinks at all."

This line of thought has more affinity with Indian philosophy than with popular Christianity.

Never the Spirit was born; the Spirit shall cease to be never;
    Never the time it was not; end and beginning are dreams.
Birthless and deathless and changeless the Spirit remaineth for ever;
    Death hath not touched it at all, dead though the house of it seems.

"God is not the God of the dead, but of the living." This is the only argument for immortality from Christ's own lips; and we cannot go much further.

June, 1939.

III

HOME

Now that I have returned from my travels "on a foreign strand," in this divine month of May, I am almost ashamed of giving my preference to the shores of the Mediterranean. "Earth has not anything to show more fair"—not than Westminster Bridge, which aroused rather excessive ecstasies in Wordsworth, but than many parts of rural England in the late spring. Why is it that Londoners view Westminster Bridge without emotion, while the Westmorland peasant wondered what Wordsworth was crooning about to himself as he trudged along under the dripping skies of the Lake District?

To me, after a quarter of a century in London, the beauty of my Berkshire home is intoxicating. Every flower-bed is gay with tulips, bluebells, and wallflowers. The foliage of the trees is still a tender green. The delicate festoons of a weeping willow dip their graceful fronds in the pool. The white spires of the chestnuts stand out against the dark leaves. The quaint red roofs of the Tudor house peep out through a riot of white and pink apple-blossom. The meadows are beginning to blaze with golden buttercups. Overhead the pale-blue sky, flecked with white clouds, is sweeter than the hard unchanging blue of the south.

I am no poet to describe these things; but I sometimes wonder why the Creator has seemingly thrown in this priceless source of happiness, for it does not seem to subserve any of the practical needs of life.

I will not discuss whether these colours and shapes are "really there," in the objects, or whether they are, in vulgar phrase, "all my eye." Beauty, I take it, is a property in things which the mind somehow recognises as akin to what is best in itself, while ugliness is what it feels to be alien, discordant, and antipathetic. The ugliest thing in nature, a human face distorted by vile passions, revolts us because the evil principle seems to have set its mark on what was meant to bear the image of God. The defacement of our beautiful country, which proceeds apace, distresses us as evidence of vulgarity and materialism.

The beautiful, says Hegel, is the spiritual making itself known sensuously. St. Augustine in a very striking sentence says, "Things above are better than things below; but all creation together is better than things above." That is to say, the revelation of God as Beauty is incomplete without its embodiment in visible form. As the Book of Genesis says, God saw the things He made, and they were good; but when He surveyed all His work together, "behold it was very good."

The words of our Lord, "consider the lilies," sanction and point the way to the whole religious poetry of Nature. The Greek Fathers lay great stress on the beauties of nature as a revelation of God.

314

And St. Francis of Assisi, the most Christlike of the saints, loved to see in everything the pulsation of one life, which sleeps in the stones, dreams in the flowers, and awakens in man. So strong was his conviction that all living things are children of God, that he would preach to his "little sisters the birds," and with quaint guilelessness undertook the conversion of "the ferocious wolf of Agobio."

Spenser, in very beautiful stanzas which are too long to quote, bids us to "read enregistered in every nook God's goodness, which His beauty doth declare, for all that's good is beautiful and fair." This may remind us of the better-known lines of Keats: "Beauty is truth, truth beauty; that is all ye know on earth and all ye need to know."

But we must not identify truth and beauty. They are two of the absolute values, or attributes of the Creator, and for man they are two paths up the hill of the Lord, which meet at the top. But we must neither confuse them nor subordinate either of them to the other.

Sir William Watson, that sadly neglected poet, puts the matter admirably:

> Forget not, brother singer, that though prose
>   Can never be too truthful, nor too wise,
> Song is not truth nor wisdom, but the rose
>   Upon truth's lips, the light in wisdom's eyes.

An important question is whether there is an absolute standard of beauty, or whether we must accept the saying that there is no disputing about tastes. Can we say dogmatically, This is beautiful, and that is ugly, however many people may think otherwise?

In my opinion, there is an absolute standard, and art, which is the wide world's memory of things, has finally decided that some things in Nature and in the works of man conform to this standard, and others do not. But the so-called practical man, who knows the price of everything and the value of nothing, who notices nothing except the things that help or hinder his personal interests, is blind to beauty. Like the pussy-cat who went to London to visit the Queen, he sees nothing except a little mouse under her chair.

Slavishness to fashion is one of the worst enemies of beauty. Think of the deformities and distortions to which women have submitted in various parts of the world and at different times. The Hottentot lady prides herself on a very large natural cushion to sit upon; steatopygia is the scientific name. The Chinese lady until quite lately had her feet bound so that she could not walk.

The Victorian lady was determined to have a waist more like a wasp than her rivals. And what can be more unpleasing than the scarlet lips and finger-nails which we see too often to-day? (From an art-glazier's advertisement—"Painted *widows*, as memorials of departed worth, have a value in the eyes of all.")

We all need some education in good taste. But if we wish to appreciate the eternal values, love or goodness, beauty and truth, we must set our affections on those goods in which one man's gain is not another man's loss, and which are open to all who will seek them with a pure heart. This is as true of beauty as of moral and scientific gains.

May, 1939.

IV

HOPES AND FEARS

DISRAELI once said, "The worst evil that one has to endure is the anticipation of calamities which never happen." Seneca put it more neatly: "He grieves more than he need who grieves before he need." I should have been a happier man if I had always observed this wise counsel.

In contrasting optimism and pessimism, we ought to remember that the optimist is often a man who whistles to keep up his courage, while the pessimist is often a man who believes in the modern beatitude: "Blessed is he who expects nothing, for he shall not be disappointed." If you lie on the ground you cannot fall any further.

Are we now making ourselves miserable by brooding over the greatest of all calamities, another world war, which perhaps is not likely to come? I am rather inclined to think so, and I fortify my opinion by reflecting on the dismal prognostications which have again and again been made at times which history tells us ought to have been full of hope.

I do not mean that optimism is always justified, or that pessimism is never justified. I am old enough just to remember that a few weeks before the outbreak of the Franco-Prussian War in 1870 a Minister of State said in Parliament that the international sky had seldom been so unclouded. And in the third century, when civilization was really crumbling, a chorus of woe proceeded from Christians and pagans alike.

Cyprian says: "The world has grown old. The rainfall and the sun's warmth are diminishing; the metals are nearly exhausted; the husbandman is failing in the fields, the sailor on the sea, the soldier in camp, honesty in the market, justice in the courts, skill in the arts, discipline in morals. This is the sentence passed upon the world, that things which have reached maturity should grow old, and that after weakness and shrinkage comes dissolution."

Tertullian says: "This is indeed the end of an Age (*ipsa clausula sæculi*) which threatens horrible misfortunes to the world." Julian in the fourth century says, "The world is at its last gasp." These gloomy prophecies were in part fulfilled; the long period between A.D. 500 and 1100 was really a dark age, barbarous and miserable.

But what periods are generally considered to have been the flowering times of civilization? Athens in the fifth and fourth centuries before Christ; the Roman Empire before the reign of Marcus Aurelius; the Renaissance, including its late bloom in Elizabethan England; and, I should certainly add, the nineteenth century. But those

319

who lived in these periods were none too happy about the future.

Pindar says that "Heaven allots two sorrows to man for every good thing." Sophocles says: "Not to be born is the best thing; the next best is to return as quickly as possible to the place from which we came." The Greeks were not habitually unhappy, but they had moods of deep depression, and they had no belief in progress.

Horace thought that his contemporaries were going from bad to worse. "The generation of our parents, worse than our grandparents, has produced us who are more worthless, and our children will be still more corrupt." Seneca says that life would be a punishment if we had not death to look forward to. Tacitus says that "our recent history proves that the gods take no thought for our happiness, but only for our punishment."

Even the jolly Elizabethans could groan very dismally. Bacon ends a lugubrious poem with "What then remains but that we still should cry not to be born, or being born to die?"

These expressions of general pessimism are less instructive for our purpose than the false predictions which were common in the nineteenth century, "the century of hope." Philosophers and men of letters were less wide of the mark than politicians and men of affairs. Matthew Arnold, George Meredith and Lord Acton all saw that Germany would be very formidable; the statesman, Sir

Charles Dilke, about 1880, enumerated the great Powers of the twentieth century; Germany was not among them.

Napoleon thought that Europe would soon be either Republican or Cossack. Wellington opined that "no sensible man doubts that England will never again be so powerful and prosperous as in the past." Mr. Joad quotes from Wellington in 1852, at the time when our country was recovering from the hungry 'forties and entering upon a period of unexampled prosperity: "I thank God I shall be spared from seeing the consummation of ruin that is gathering about us."

The two following quotations are from the same source. Wilberforce, the reformer, declared: "I dare not marry; the future is so unsettled." (He afterwards recovered his spirits sufficiently to marry a member of my wife's family.) In 1849 Disraeli said: "In industry, commerce and agriculture there is no hope." He was then in Opposition.

It seems that we are all very bad judges of what is going to happen. How many people fifty years ago foretold the fate of democracy? Amiel did, in 1852: "Materialism is the auxiliary doctrine of every tyranny. To crush the spiritual human man by specializing him; to create not human beings but wheels for the great social machine; to enslave the soul of things, to de-personalize man is the dominant tendency of our epoch. What is threatened is moral liberty, the very nobility of man."

One or two general reflections may conclude this article. There is of course no law of progress, and if, as many have thought, history shows an advance not in a straight line but in a spiral, it also shows that, in Tennyson's phrase, "many a backward-streaming curve" has interrupted the ascent.

There is however good reason to hope that if we take long views, changes will be found to be on the whole for the better, and it is almost certain that if, as science thinks probable, our race is nearer its beginning than its end, there will be flowering times of genius and achievement in the future not less glorious than in the past.

Belief in temporal progress is not an integral part of Christianity, and we must not hope that Providence will save us from the consequences of our moral and intellectual errors. But faith will help us to bear our troubles, and to believe that they will always be bearable. In the truly religious mind there is an ultimate optimism which gives courage to overcome superficial pessimism:

> Eternity, be thou my refuge.

May, 1939.

V

NATURE'S HANDICAPS

DEMOCRACY, which is the fictitious equality of
unequals, and Socialism, which offers to reward
everyone according to his needs, not according to
the value of his services, cannot go very far to
redress Nature's handicaps.

One man is born with a silver spoon in his mouth,
another with a millstone round his neck. There are
faces which are an open letter of recommendation
and others which repel those who look at them. One
man has the best reason for being happy—namely,
that he is so; another has to struggle all his life with
mental depression. One has a disposition so happily
attuned that we might think that the devil has
forgotten him; another is plagued with various tempt-
ations for which he cannot reasonably blame himself.

There are compensations, no doubt. George
Borrow, the author of *Lavengro*, says in a remarkable
passage that the unhappy, who have a spur which
will not let them rest, go further than the cheerful,
who are content with what life has given them.
Ambition, "the last infirmity of noble minds," is
sometimes the recreation of the fortunate and sometimes the distraction of the sufferer. The last is
the strongest spur, at any rate in early life, when the
foundations of success are being laid.

Of all natural handicaps, mental derangement is the worst. We sometimes talk of happiness as the greatest good; but which of us would like to change places with a cheerful lunatic who fancies that he is Alexander the Great?

But how many people are perfectly sane? How many have all their values right? Some are vain and make themselves ridiculous. Others are proud and rebuff those who wish to be friends with them. I have known men who have ruined their own happiness and poisoned the atmosphere round them by brooding savagely over the injustice which they fancy has been done to them—a sort of Ishmael complex, as if their hand was against everyone and everyone's hand against them.

There are also the merely stupid, a very large class. Do we always remember that weakness of the intelligence deserves as much pity as weakness of the body? A Prime Minister said that before appointing a bishop he would like to ask him one question: "Will you suffer fools gladly?" It is a searching question for us all.

When St. Paul tells us to bear one another's burdens, we should understand it as referring to moral burdens as well as money troubles and the like. It is an elementary duty of a Christian to do his best to make his neighbours behave rather less badly than they are at present disposed to do. This principle will carry us a long way. Among other things, we should be careful not to put the other fellow entirely in the wrong, if we want to be friends with him afterwards.

Next to mental failure, blindness is surely the worst of afflictions. By far the greater part of our contacts with the external world comes to us through sight. When people say, as they do sometimes, that total deafness must be worse than blindness, they forget that the deaf man forgets his infirmity when he is alone, and that there are sadly few things that the blind man can do in solitude.

Nevertheless, human courage and heroism never rise to a greater height than in the efforts of the blind to overcome their misfortune.

If I were asked to choose the finest piece of poetry, not only in English but in any language, I should name without hesitation the first fifty-six lines of the third book of Milton's *Paradise Lost,* beginning "Hail, holy light." He does not extenuate his loss:

> Not to me returns
> Day, or the sweet approach of even or morn,
> Or sight of vernal bloom, or summer's rose,
> Or flocks or herds or human face divine;

and "wisdom at one entrance quite shut out." But at once he ends:

> So much the rather thou celestial Light
> Shine inward, and the mind through all her powers
> Irradiate, there plant eyes, all mist from thence
> Purge and disperse, that I may see and tell
> Of things invisible to mortal sight.

The sublime dignity of these lines almost quenches pity.

I have had the privilege of knowing one blind lady, Miss Madeline Horsfall, to whose book of essays I wrote a preface. It was her way to speak and write as if she saw; and she really seemed to see, with a fine discrimination and delicate humour.

Tennyson was very short-sighted. Did he really see all the natural objects which he describes so well? Sometimes the short-sighted come to their own in old age. I remember seeing an old lady of ninety-five reading a badly printed newspaper without spectacles. I could not help congratulating her. She told me that she had been very short-sighted, but that her eyeballs were now just of the right shape.

Beethoven is said to have been too deaf to hear his own music. I believe great musicians can read a score with as much pleasure as we can read poetry in silence.

The story of Helen Keller is an amazing example of how even the double infirmity of blindness and deafness may be overcome by patience, courage and intelligence. Such a combination of afflictions is fortunately very rare.

In old age we no longer think of bodily troubles as handicaps, for we are out of the running. "The years as they pass," says Horace, who was not really an old man, "rob us of everything, one by one; they have torn from me merriment, love, dinners and games; they threaten to wring from me my poetry." Well, if we are wise we do not grumble; there will not be much more to give up when our call comes.

If life is a race, who are the winners? That is not for us to say. Penn's "No Cross, no Crown" is echoed by secular writers. Plato says, "Without pain it is impossible to get rid of sin." We may be sure that what we call handicaps are taken into account in adjudging the final award.

Those who to our eyes have been most successful have not been too well satisfied with their own performances. One could hardly find two more outwardly successful careers than those of Goethe and Bismarck. Yet both of them have testified that they enjoyed very few happy days.

Shakespeare speaks of the day of his death as "that well-contented day." "Well, the game is over, and I am not sorry," were the last words of the Duke of Devonshire, the statesman.

As for some grossly successful men, we neither know nor care whether they were satisfied with themselves or not.

But one reflection clearly emerges. Since there are very many to whom life has not been kind, we ought not to make things worse for each other.

August, 1939.

VI

A PAGAN SAINT

WHAT are the great ideals, the ultimate values, to the service of which we may properly devote our lives? Philosophers tell us that the supreme values are goodness, truth and beauty. Suggestions to add a fourth, such as life, or happiness, have not been received with favour.

Dr. C. E. M. Joad calls them the three dowagers, implying that in becoming eminently respectable they have lost the freshness of youth. But the dowagers still occupy their seats of honour, although they are not much in favour with the man-in-the-street, for whom all values are instrumental.

What, he asks, is the use of the saint, who aims at goodness, the scientist and philosopher, who seek after truth, and the poet or artist, who worships beauty?

Why, none, from his point of view. These are not instrumental values; they must be served for their own sake or not at all. However, they alone make life worth living.

One of them combats moral evil, one ignorance, one ugliness.

It is a queer mistake to suppose that science studies facts and is indifferent to values. It really devotes itself to one of the three ultimate values, truth, and neglects for its own purposes the moral and æsthetic aspects of reality. It does not take all knowledge for its province—that is the task of philosophy—but one kind of knowledge.

In the whole-hearted service of truth it has produced authentic saints, that is to say, wholly disinterested men and women, who are as worthy of homage as the great mystics and philosophers and poets.

The Life of Madame Marie Curie, who, in collaboration with her husband, Pierre Curie, as devoted and almost as brilliant as herself, discovered radium, has been justly described as a great book about a great genius. It is also unquestionably the biography of a saint—a saint who did not believe in God.

Religion never touched her or her husband, and when Pierre, absent-minded student as he was, was run over and killed in the streets of Paris, his widow never even doubted that death is utter and final extinction.

Goethe says that "he who has science and art has also religion." For Goethe science and art were religion. This splendid old pagan is one of the greatest names in European literature; but our countrymen have never admired him wholeheartedly. He never let himself go. In "building up the pyramid of his existence," to use his own phrase, many of the bricks were women's lives. His interest in religion was only intellectual, and he had no taste for martyrdom in any cause.

Charles Darwin once wrote (I quote from memory), "It is a cursed thing to be so wrapped up in any pursuit as I am in mine." He regrets that he has lost his interest in poetry and other things. Rather too much has been made of this admission, which might have been made by any specialist on the track of a great discovery.

We cannot do much good in any one line without giving up many other things which we should have liked to do and to be. Fortunately, any worthy pursuit takes on a kind of universality; a broad mind is not much cramped by a narrow sphere.

The remarkable thing about Madame Curie is that having put her hand to the plough she never once looked back. And yet she was not a narrow or one-sided genius. As a young child she showed a precocious talent for languages. She was a first-rate mathematician. She was a good mother, and she made herself a good cook and housekeeper.

In the Great War she proved that she had remarkable organizing ability, which she used in hospital work, very inadequately recognized by the French Government. But with iron determination she concentrated her whole wonderful talent upon the work which she had chosen.

It was almost a chance that she chose for her life's work the further development of Röntgen's and Becquerel's discoveries. She had to struggle with desperate poverty, and since nobody would provide the Curies with a decent laboratory, their experiments were made in a miserable shed.

They were further handicapped by the jealousy and incredulity of the French savants, who at one time nearly broke her stubborn spirit by calumny and hostility. This is a very unpleasant chapter in the book; we may be glad that Lord Kelvin and other British scientists were always her admiring friends.

The hardest part of her work was the task, successful after years of exhausting labour, of isolating pure radium from the ore in which it was embedded, and determining its atomic weight. Till this was done, the incredulity of the French chemists was insuperable. But no sooner had she won this triumph—the credit belongs to her, for Pierre was discouraged and half inclined to give up the attempt —than it was discovered that radium is sometimes very successful in the treatment of cancer.

At once the discovery was worth a large fortune to its inventors. It was necessary only to take out a patent, for the Curies alone possessed the secret. But they agreed without hesitation to make a present of their discovery to the world. It was not in accordance with the honour of science to make money out of a medical discovery.

Their only regret was that with the help of money they might have installed a properly equipped laboratory, and perhaps radium institutes, such as now exist in several countries.

331

Absolute disinterestedness is the note of Madame Curie's life, and is not this the mark of what Catholics call heroic virtue? We may no doubt find similar self-devotion in a crank or political *enragé*, whose activities are either absurd or mischievous. It is necessary, for lay canonization, that the life should be devoted to some worthy object—in fact, as I said at the beginning of my essay, to one of Dr. Joad's three dowagers.

There are, then, three ways up the hill of the Lord, which meet only at the top. Madame Curie, William Wordsworth and St. John of the Cross, the Spanish mystic, may seem very unlike each other, and the first and third would not have had much common ground.

But "in my Father's house are many mansions." The mind of God is too vast for any one human mind to grasp. Self-surrender to some great quest; the search for the Holy Grail, whether this is thought of as perfect Truth or perfect Goodness or perfect Beauty—it is to this that the noblest spirits are called; and it is such men and women who have done most to make the world a better place.

September, 1938.

332